Be Seen,
Be Heard,
Get Paid
What
You Are
Worth

DAVID ROYLANCE

Publisher

HCB Publishing Ltd.
London, United Kingdom

Printed in EU, UK, Canada and the
United States of America

ISBN: 978-1-3999-1919-7

Connect with the author:

david@speaktoshine.uk
www.speaktoshine.uk
+44(0)203 740 5939
+44(0)777 046 5149

Exclusive Offer

I want you, the reader, to achieve the most it is possible to achieve through reading this book. As you will discover, I, and my brilliant team of experts, regularly help our clients to achieve promotions that add an extra £100–£300,000 into their income stream. Lives are transformed with the addition of that level of income. I am also pleased to say that my clients, via promotion, have used their considerable skills and values to upskill and improve the lives of fellow co-workers, customers and stakeholders.

In this book, I will run with you through the process as I would with a client taking a journey of 6 months or more with me. It's easier and quicker to receive those results when you have someone like me running next to you, sometimes holding your hand, and sometimes kicking your butt into action!

Although this book will show you how to achieve that promotion, I can't make the promise that it will happen exclusively through reading this book.

I have, however, had a client achieve a promotion through having a complimentary strategy call with me.

That is why I have created some extra content for you to use over and above the resource you have in your hand.

Follow this link for exclusive extra material I have prepared for you as the reader of this book.

https://www.davidroylance.com/secret-book-chapter

Dedication

To my extraordinary wife, Emma, and my children, Maisie and Bertie. Emma, thank you for your dedication to our love and us as a family, never giving in, always striving to create more for us all. I am more grateful to the Universe than you know, that you and I were pointed toward each other and found love.

Maisie, thank you for showing me what an incredible, powerful, articulate, passionate and beautiful young woman you are.

Bertie, or Albert if you are feeling formal, thank you for always being fun to be with, your irrepressible personality and your dedication to advancing yourself. Stay tenacious. You are well on your way to becoming a successful, generous and happy man.

To my brilliant sister, Alison Roylance-White and her husband Chalky White. The Roylances have always been a breed apart, and thank goodness for that! You looked after me when I was broken, stayed with me until mended, and have been a constant source of resourcefulness and love for me and my family.

To my mother and father, both sadly gone from this world, who showed me how to stand up for values worth inhabiting. Thank you for my upbringing. Thank you for the generosity and love you gave to me and my sister. I think of you both every day. I grow more appreciative of everything you did with every milestone I achieve in my life.

Thank you to my closest friends, my mentors, my best family at my wedding and now my business partners, Chris and Karene Lambert-Gorwyn. Thank you also to Mya Lambert-Gorwyn. Your generosity knows no bounds. You have shown me the way. You have picked me up when I have fallen. You have held my hand and led me in times of trouble. You all have extraordinary minds and hearts. Your familial commitment to making others' lives better has been an inspiration for me. Thank you also to Goldie the dog, who always comes to me when I visit.

To David Gil Cristobal, my friend, and my business partner. You are the best "ideas" man I have ever met. Over the last 2 years we have met regularly on Zoom. You are the most fun, and a massive inspiration for me.

To Anna Goodwin, who is always there for me when I need to talk. Like everyone else, I have wobbly moments. In the same way that I can shine a light for others, I find that sometimes I can't see my blind spots. Anna, thank you for being my friend.

To Amy and Simon Rogers, thank you. Amy, thank you for being the boss of me when I needed it. Simon, thank you for kindness and determination to share your amazing gifts to the world.

To all my associate team, thank you. I love you all and appreciate your individual gifts.

Katya Benjamin, thank you. I am amazed I get to share my clients with the woman who taught me the Alexander Technique when I was at Drama School.

To Beth Redfern, you have been amazing at creating the life you wanted. You bring your love of your skill to my clients, enhancing their lives every time. You are a star.

To Tara Sutton, watching you grow as a person and as a practitioner has been a joy and a greatly satisfying experience. Now you share your journey in a way that moves others forward. That is something to be proud of.

To Koosje Kosters, thank you. It was a blast when we were working together. I loved watching you present to my Dutch clients in Dutch. Your infectious energy is wonderful. I am super happy you are in this world, spreading the love.

To everyone in the team at Heart Centred Business. I have supported you and you have supported me. Every one of you brings something unique and valuable to my life and my business. Thank you, Sarah, Jane, Sharon, Hayley, Hetty, Nicola and Jade.

To every one of my clients, thank you. Whether we worked together one to one or in a group setting, thank you. Every success has been a joy, every challenge has been a great opportunity to learn and become better at what I do.

To Patsy Rodenburg, thank you. The greatest teacher in the world of the voice. Your influence is much larger than you know. Thank you for teaching me. Thank you for the time you devoted to helping me when I was hurting, whilst at Guildhall School.

To Vasily Skorik, thank you. Sadly, Vasily is no longer in this world. He showed me what is possible as a director of people. As a theatre director he could see and hear exactly what an actor needed to know, yet he didn't speak a word of English. From Vasily I learned to look and listen for that which is really important. Our time together in Tuscany is a memory to be treasured.

To Kane and Alessia Minkus, who were there at the beginning of my journey and for introducing me to Chris and Karene Lambert-Gorwyn.

To Jennie Koo from the WIBF (Women in Banking and Finance) who has been an incredible advocate for me and my business and helped gain access to many more people who I have helped, whether they become a client or not.

To Dr Jordan B Peterson. We shook hands when I attended your lecture in London. Your writings and your videos have been cornerstones in helping me move forward and help others move forward. Thank you also for introducing me to Understand Myself.

To Ben Lionel Scott for your amazing videos that have kept me focused and productive on the days I don't feel like it.

To Sir Roger Moore and Peter Wyngarde, the 2 actors I met in my lifetime who oozed presence and charisma like no others. In your onscreen worlds you showed me, from a young age, that masculinity and respect stood as values side by side. I was lucky enough to see Sir Roger in his last public appearance before his death, when he taught me never to give up on anybody. I was also lucky enough to work with Peter rehearsing for a play in Regents Park. Peter's voice remains the gold standard of beautiful voices. Both of you have proven to have values that I have and continue to aspire to.

Foreword

Crossing paths with someone who is passionate about helping others succeed is enormously refreshing, unexpected, great even. But meeting someone who is prepared to share the entirety of their wisdom and knowledge, without reservation, with the single motivation to help others succeed, is nothing short of amazing. That is David Roylance.

I first met David through my volunteer work with Women in Banking & Finance (WiBF). At that time, his laudable mission to reach 1,000 women with his work was in its infancy. David's aim, through his voice, leadership and presentation coaching, is to empower 1,000 women to use their voices effectively.

From that day forward, having shown us all the merest glimpse of his brilliance, David became an ongoing supporter of WiBF. In fact, I was delighted to note that he was named in the 40for40 "Friend of WiBF" category, as part of its 40th anniversary celebrations. 40for40 showcases some of the greatest supporters and advocates of WiBF, whose contributions personify its positive impact. David fits brilliantly into that niche.

David has since become a bestselling author and continues to return to WiBF to support our members in his own unique style - it isn't about 'fixing' women or turning them into alpha females. Instead, David focuses on encouraging women to stand up and be counted in their own style. He reminds us that we should all be investing ourselves – after all, he says, if we were a business we'd be investing in assets or developing new products, so why are our careers and livelihoods any different?

I don't mind admitting that my ability to invest in myself didn't come easily at all at the start of my career. In fact, it seemed unnatural, counterproductive even. Because investing in yourself is about giving yourself downtime to reflect and work on your mental wellbeing (something that David talks about in this book), not just developing academic and technical knowledge.

If I'm honest downtime was usually at the very bottom of my to do list. I'd get to it after I'd done everything else …or not at all. After all, if I was getting all my work done to an exceptional quality, that would be enough, right?

The reality is, while there are leaders who will praise and even seek out those willing to work their knuckles to the bone, hard work alone will only get you so far. …And that is often to the detriment of a whole host of other, very important, things – such as family, relationships, and 'me time'.

I realised that in order to change this potentially destructive cycle and succeed in my financial services career, I not only needed to invest in myself, I needed to find my voice and actually be heard.

But finding my voice was not easy. I battled for years with being told I was either 'not speaking up enough' or being 'too outspoken'. Striking that delicate balance was a challenge in itself, but overlay my Chinese heritage, and its ingrained traditions that include respecting your elders (which means never challenging them), and you have an even more complicated path to navigate. Throw in the imposter syndrome that sometimes rears its ugly head, and you have the myriad of forces I was (and sometimes still am) fighting against.

So why is being seen and being heard for the right reasons so difficult? The trouble is, we still live in an era where certain behaviours and associated attributes, can be regarded as positive by some and negative by others, depending entirely on who is displaying the behaviour. Take being assertive and proactive as examples… fantastic attributes for a male, but as a female, they make you 'bossy' and 'pushy'.

Or take compassionate and reflective – positive qualities, right? Not necessarily. As a female that makes you 'emotional' 'weak' or 'indecisive'.

This gendered language unfortunately very much still exists – albeit mostly as an subconscious norm' for how we view others. Subconscious or not though, it can have a significant impact both mentally and professionally for those on the receiving end. Trust me, I know.

For those receiving this 'feedback', it can be unhelpful, unconstructive and hurtful. In fact, all you really want to do is retreat and resign yourself to the fact that your career dreams are just not meant to be.

And gendered language is (sadly) going nowhere fast. The situation is definitely improving, but this way of thinking is still extremely prevalent, if not rife.

I've lost count of the number of mentees who have told me that if they speak up in the same way as their male peers, they are either dismissed offhand, or worse still, branded as 'difficult'.

I similarly lose count of the number of women who have been promised a promotion, only to be offered sideways moves as a pacifier, whilst those around them are accelerated, whilst delivering much less. Welcome to 2022?

But this is where David's work steps in, to help identify and release your *true* value. This isn't a one-size-fits-all approach, but it is about working with your individual circumstances to find your true self – and being comfortable with it – in order to fully find your voice.

This approach, combined with understanding the impact of your presence, not just on your audience but on yourself, has seen numerous senior females become the best version of themselves, accelerating them into greater roles but also making them significantly happier, having discovered their worth.

David's style is both energetic and engaging. Even in a virtual setting with a large audience, it's difficult to come away from one of his workshops without a new-found lease of determination …and this book is no different.

You'll find the words will leap out at you, energising you to think differently, whilst guiding you to take positive action to enable you to be the best version of yourself.

This book is for anyone who wants to be seen and heard for the right reasons. Turn the page and get started with a new approach to being seen, heard and recognised for your true worth.

Jennie Koo
Banking & Finance Risk Professional and
Women in Banking & Finance – Head of Branches.

Introduction

Hello, dear reader.

My name is David Roylance. I am known as Europe's No 1 Smasher of the Glass Ceiling because I help my clients, the majority of whom are ambitious women, to smash the glass ceiling in their chosen industry.

I'm not going to spend a lot of words on an introduction because I will be revealing so much about my life and experience in the book proper. I'm writing this introduction having already written the book and being very excited about the content and the stories I am sharing.

My private clients pay me £50,000 to work with me. They do this because they have a significant desire in their lives that will reward them tenfold to the amount they have invested. Because of that level of investment, it means that I can only work with 7 people a year at that level.

Yet, I would much rather that the content and stories that I share with them had a much wider audience. I know that if more people in this world understood how important it is to be connected to their value and stand by and live into their values daily, the world would ultimately be a much happier, more fulfilled place.

I love people. I just love people. I love seeing people do well. I love seeing people do well by each other. I love making people's lives better.

That is why, earlier last year, I started putting fingertip to laptop.

Here is a little bit of information about me before we get going.

I was born in Edinburgh in 1963. I had a lovely upbringing with parents who adored me and my fabulous younger sister.

We were both fortunate to have strong role models (though I massively disagreed with them as a revolutionary, artistic teenager) who understood the value of work and creating a legacy for both of us.

In my life I have been a hi-fi salesman (my first Saturday job as a teen), an outreach worker teaching drama to the disadvantaged, an actor, a theatre director, a presentation coach, a manager of a series of mobile phone shops, a man in a giant rabbit costume selling breakfast cereal, a telesales person, a barman and a business coach, which is where I found my calling in life to help others make massive changes in their lives. The most obvious massive change is the huge upscale in income. The biggest change is in who my clients become in the journey. Taller, stronger, and more confident.

Onstage, I was a Russian nobleman, a one legged Restoration fop, a fish, Billy the Kid, every nobleman in Scotland smooshed (a technical term) into one character (in an adaptation of Macbeth), a silent movie Hollywood dancer and many spear carriers at the back of the stage (where I learned my acting craft from watching others be brilliant).

As a theatre director I have been mentored by the best in the world, from Yukio Ninagawa in Japan to Vasilij Skorik from Russia, to the world's number 1 voice coach Patsy Rodenburg who personally coached me to understand and do justice to the greatest storyteller the world has known, William Shakespeare. With their help I became an exceptional actor and an even better theatre director.

When working in the theatre I had confidence in my ability to act and direct, and none in myself personally. I refused to market myself. As a result, the best parts and the most money went to those who would. I bought into, at the time, the toxic internal stories that keep the largest percentage of actors in a state of "virtuous" penury.

Just imagine what you could do for the world if you were more confident, and that confidence encouraged you to take action. I really mean that. Take a moment right now, before you go on with the book to ask yourself what you would do with your life if you felt more confident.

I live in Hampshire now, a county I love because it affords me time in the outdoors and breathe a beautiful air in a way I never did when I was in London. I owe my sanity and my reason to live, and live better, to my wife, Emma, and my children, Maisie and Bertie, who provide me with accountability, love and laughs. I am determined to help my children be the strongest, independent beings that they deserve to be.

In this book I am going to share with you everything I have shared with my clients. All of the techniques and exercises that I share and work with my clients. My clients add between £100–£300,000 on average into their income stream through putting these exercises into action.

With no further ado, I am going to let you get into the book proper. Writing it has brought up all sorts of emotions. The feeling that matters the most is the joy of sharing.

It's a pleasure to share this with you. I wish you joy and satisfaction reading it.

Table of Contents

Chapter 1: Presence

Be present in yourself – have
presence for other people

*You have to be at home with yourself
in order to be seen as confident.*

Presence is a word that many people use, and few have any idea what it means. It is bandied about in the corporate world as if it is a form of magic, usually by people who believe they possess it. If "presence" is a magical construct then surely the people who have it are in control of deciding who else does and does not have it.

It is not unusual for these people, predominately men, to exercise judgement over others using the idea of "presence" or "charisma". After all, being able to point at someone and say "He has it" or "She doesn't" creates power around that person. It also creates power around the magical ingredient that is "presence". If it is magical, then there is nothing a person can do to have it if they feel they don't.

Working with my clients at Speak to Shine, the first thing I am keen to dispel is the myth that "presence" has any magic about it.

The irony is that most people think that presence is something you must put on, like an item of clothing. Those who wish to have it will seek to find ways to fake it as per the maxim "fake it 'til you make it". As a result, many put on a show of charisma that audiences see through immediately as an acting performance. Acting performances that can be spotted are inauthentic by their nature.

It is easy to have presence when you are in your comfort zone.

Would you agree with me if I said that there are times in your life when you can operate with ease and effortlessly? Would you also agree that you sometimes enter situations in life when, perhaps because they are unfamiliar circumstances, or there may be a desirable outcome associated with this circumstance, that you suddenly find yourself unable to do with ease that which you would ordinarily be able to do? When we have those experiences, typically we find ourselves frightened of others being able to see that we are nervous. The next logical step is to do everything in our power to disguise our discomfort, because we believe that others seeing our vulnerability means they see weakness. So, we put on a performance.

For years I put on my own performance in the hope that people would not "find me out". I did that until I met the woman who became my first mentor, though I did not realise it at the time.

Patsy Rodenburg is, without doubt, the world's number 1 voice coach. I say this writing in the world in 2021. When I met her in 1990, I was an introverted 27-year-old from Edinburgh who believed that he needed to put on a performance to be interesting to others. I held my shoulders high, smoked Gauloise cigarettes because I thought it made me look poetic, and hid behind a slope of blonde hair that fell covering my right eye and half my face. Patsy was the first to be direct and tell me that I was putting on a performance. For the first time it hit me that by putting on this show I was limiting how I could make an impact in the world.

Patsy taught me that you have to be present in yourself, in order to have presence for others. That meant that you must be comfortable in your own skin. A person must breathe into their own skin, be physically comfortable through the way they breathe.

Presence and leadership are both positions of vulnerability. Vulnerability is strength.

I remember listening to a radio broadcast of a Superbowl. 2 former players were discussing the game during a break. They were talking about one quarterback player in glowing terms. One said, "Fear is not in his vocabulary!" to which the other replied, "That must make him a very stupid person."

We cannot be brave if we do not understand what it is to feel fear. If we feel no fear, then there is nothing to step over, no way we can grow. The magic of personal growth happens when we are out of our comfort zone. We choose to become better and more competent.

To be present when one is afraid or out of one's comfort zone is to be brave.

To be present is to be comfortable in one's skin. To operate effortlessly in one's own body despite the fear.

To be present is to breathe with comfort, preferably in the stomach. Breathing into our core will mean that the whole body operates as a unit and that the brain is fully oxygenated. By this I mean that oxygen is fully distributed throughout the entirety of your brain.

Human beings are naturally rapport building creatures. They mirror each other all the time, in almost all the easy conversations and communications we have with each other.

When people are in groups, for instance an audience to a presentation, or round a boardroom table, then they react in the same way as they would do in a one-to-one conversation. People seek to build rapport with the most dominant, or the most present*, person in the room. One of the most basic methods of building rapport is to synchronize our breath patterns. We will seek to breathe in the same pattern as that person who is most dominant, or most present.

That is why I am suggesting you must be present in yourself in order to have presence for other people.

---

* To be clear, I am suggesting that dominant is not necessarily the same thing as present. I think most of us know what it like to be led in a room by someone who is dominant and not at all present.

If Barack Obama Can Do It So Can You

*Anyone can achieve any level
of confidence they want*

This is a pretty big statement, right?

I mean it too. If Barack Obama can take one of the most powerful jobs in the world, then so can you.

Here is the thing. People often make the presumption that because Barack Obama is one of the most natural presences in front of a camera and standing on a stage – in front of huge audiences – this means that he has always been a natural. After all, as I said earlier, people assume that presence is a "magical" quality. Either we have it or we don't.

I remember seeing an audience with Sir Roger Moore, on the South Bank in London, just months before he sadly left us. People assumed that because he was so charming that he was born with it, that it was totally natural. Nothing could be further from the truth. He was born to a working-class family, his father a police constable, in Stockwell, London. He was lucky enough to be handsome enough to model and get picked up by a scout from MGM in the early 1950s, who took him to America, and he became an actor contracted to MGM. He began his acting career in film playing small parts in movies. During his first film, the director, who was massively frustrated by the way he was showing up on camera, sent him to what was in those days referred to as a dialogue coach. Nowadays this would be known as a voice coach. His voice coach asked him this; "You are 6ft 3. Why are you standing 5ft 9?" Sir Roger realised he was denying his height, seeking unconsciously to be smaller than he was. Once he learnt how to stand to his full height, and be vulnerable enough to be properly "seen", his life changed. "I stood at 6ft 3, and I became the hero. And I have been playing the hero ever since" he said.

When Barack Obama left university he was told in no uncertain terms "Do not get a job that involves any kind of public speaking! You are terrible." Funnily enough, Bill Clinton was given the same message when he left university. Yes, being able to speak with presence and charisma does not seem to have harmed either of their careers.

We make presumptions about people when we see or hear them appearing so natural whilst in pressurised situations or speaking in front of big audiences. The presumption we make is that they must have always been like that. Not many people imagine the work that has made all of that possible.

What I am here to say is that both men faced a moment when they realised there was a job they wanted, and their desire to achieve that role meant that they were willing to do whatever it took to make sure they were successful. They learned how to appear natural and then practised it until it was true.

What was it they learned then?

Try this exercise.

Think of a person who you feel has "presence". It could be someone who you know, someone you work with, someone you have seen on television or a cinema screen. It could be someone from the world of politics. It could be someone from the world of personal development.

It doesn't matter who you choose. What matters is this is someone you believe has "presence".

Close your eyes and run a movie in your mind's eye. This movie stars the person you have selected. Observe them in action. Perhaps they are speaking from a stage. Perhaps they are leading a meeting. Perhaps they are motivating a team.

Ask yourself this question as you run your movie. "What is it they are DOING that means you believe them to have 'presence'?"

Good. Now write down your answers.

When I have had audiences do this exercise with me, they often say things like: "They appear confident"; or "They have authority". Great. They probably do, however that does not help us. Both of those statements are judgements. The audience judges whether someone has confidence or authority. We make those judgements based on actions those people are taking.

So, again, I ask my audience the question: "What are they doing that means you make those judgements?" Now we start to drill down into useful feedback.

"They are standing absolutely straight." "They speak really slowly and clearly." "They have a very deep voice."

Now we are getting somewhere. Now we are beginning to get feedback that is worth having.

Change the Way That You Are Experienced by Others

You are more in charge than you think

Now we know that the focus for change should start at behaviour. What are you physically doing to create the experience that others are having around you? Because most of us never ask these questions, they never change their circumstances and relationships, strained or otherwise, and stay the same as they always have done. How many times have you had work colleagues exclaim, "They (the other, difficult, person) are just the way they are, and I am the way I am. Nothing is going to change."

If you don't believe change is possible, why is any human being going to try. Right?

Have you ever asked yourself the question "What values do others see in me when I am in the room?"

When I am working with my private clients I often send them back into their workplace to ask that question of their colleagues and bosses. For many, it confronts a real fear. What if the answer is "nothing"? It has never happened to a client yet, and I dare say it never will.

One of our most basic fears as human beings is rejection. Fear of rejection brings the hypothalamus into play. The hypothalamus is the part of the back end of your brain, often referred to as the monkey brain, or the reptile brain. Its job is to do whatever it needs to do to keep you alive. The hypothalamus is a simple part of the brain. It can accomplish 3 thoughts. Shall I hit them (the other person or people identified as a threat)? Shall I run away? Shall I pretend that I am dead?

Anything more complex than those thoughts needs to be done in the frontal lobe of the brain. The frontal lobe of the brain can only function when oxygen is flowing fully through it. When the hypothalamus senses danger, which it does by monitoring our heart rate – which is defined by whether we are breathing in the chest or the stomach – it steals all the oxygen from the frontal lobe and stores it in the back of the brain for you to do that "hit", "run" or "pretend I am dead" response. Since the hypothalamus hasn't evolved since the Stone Age, it does not know the difference between a sabre-toothed tiger chasing you and a presentation. It identifies that you are in a state of fear, and acts accordingly.

In the Stone Age, rejection by your tribe would mean being left in the cold to die. That is why so many of us fear finding out what others genuinely experience as a value from us.

Asking that question in relation to "values" is step number 1.

Once we know what values people already experience of you, then I ask my clients to identify 3 values that you would like people to experience of you. Most often it is "higher credibility" or "integrity" that come up for clients.

That is step 2.

Step 3 is to think of a person who inhabits these values already. Then together we run the same exercise as I described above where we watch a video in our mind's eye of this person in action and we ask the question, "What is it they are doing that means I believe they are this value?"

My exercise here for you is this.

- Think of 3 values you would like people to see in you.
- Think of a person, preferably a different person for each value.
- Run a movie in your mind's eye of your person in action.

What is it they are doing that means you are experiencing this value?

Write down the answers.

Once you have found replicable behaviour, you can do something yourself to change the way others experience you.

Be Pleased to be There – Wherever You Are

John F Kennedy had a secret to his confidence

You are the only person who is going to have your journey in life. You are the only person who is going to live exactly like you.

Be yourself then. Everyone else is taken.

It is a liberating thought to realise that comparison with other people is a hopeless endeavour. I am a great believer in having heroes. That is, people who have done in life something like that which you want to do, or people who clearly reveal values that matter to you in life. It is always good to have someone to chase. Aim at someone who has more of what you want than you do now.

The only person you should compare yourself with is who you were in the past. This is Rule No. 2 in Jordan Peterson's

12 Rules For Life (*12 Rules for Life: An Antidote to Chaos*: Amazon.co.uk: Peterson, Jordan B.: 9780241351635: Books). Can you honestly look back at who you were yesterday or the day before and say that today you are a better person, or today you have taken a step to making your life more like the life you want to live? If not, how come? Who do you want to be?

I mention this because there are 2 ways of looking at everything life throws at you. Life throws some difficult stuff for us all to contend with. I cannot imagine there isn't a full life lived which hasn't contained some massive upheaval in either personal or societal change.

The 2 ways of looking at life are: Why is this happening TO me? Why is this happening FOR me? Notice how those 2 questions inspire different kinds of thinking in the brain. The first leads us into the past with the suggestion that problems are not here to be circumnavigated. The first leads us into the area that we, personally, are being punished for some reason. It also leads us down the rabbit hole of resentment. Resentment that others are not having the same experience as you. Resentment is one of the most dangerous emotions to be experienced.

The second question inspires different thinking. What am I here to learn? Where is the learning in the experience? What do I need to step over the challenge? What am I missing here? How do I make sure this never happens again?

The second question inspires your growth mindset.

This means, whatever happens to you, no matter how appalling the circumstances, how might your life change if you asked the second question of yourself, rather than the first?

Try this now.

If you are in the middle of a challenge in your life, use this. If not, then perhaps roleplay a challenge that you stepped over in your life. Ask yourself the second question and see what comes up. Write down your answers. Then hold yourself accountable to the learning you come up with.

What if you were pleased to be here, regardless of the circumstance? What if that is what you chose?

John F Kennedy called this "The Cocktail State". He loved a cocktail party and being at a cocktail party was his preferred physical, mental and emotional state. He was always pleased to be there.

When John began the long process of standing to be President of the United States he found himself attending many functions at which it was necessary for him to speak. At first he found these speeches made him extremely nervous and his performance when nervous was less than stellar.

Then he created the idea of the "Cocktail State". The Cocktail State would be the optimum state to be in. At parties he would function effortlessly, charmingly and with the maximum of presence. Heads would turn when he entered a room. People would smile and swoon over him. How could he feel like that when he was doing these speeches?

He went out of his way to educate his brain and body that he was pleased to be there.

Before each reception he would peek through the curtains or door without the people in the room seeing him. He would look at individuals in the room and say – out loud – to himself, "I'm glad I'm here. I'm glad you're here. I'm glad I'm here with you."

He would repeat this mantra with several people he was laying his eyes on. He repeated it until he felt it in his body that it was true.

When he felt it, he pulled back the curtain and moved into the room

Be glad you're here. Be glad the people you love are here. Be glad you are here with them.

Return of Investment in Yourself

*Invest in yourself when you need it,
regardless of circumstance, it will
come back to you later tenfold*

This is advice. Most people will never heed this. The reason most people never will is the scarcity mindset that sits in their head.

A scarcity mindset is based on the idea that whatever it is they want in life, they cannot afford it. The fear that is there is only a certain amount of money in the world, and that only a few of us can have it. This fear of "the lack of" stops people taking advantage of opportunity. People don't invest in themselves, miss opportunity and get stuck in their circumstances.

All of us have a choice. We can choose to be bigger than our circumstances, or not. The choice is in how we approach this in the mind. Is this a problem that stops us, or is this a challenge we can find a way over?

You get to choose, every time.

Everyone I have ever met who needed to invest in themselves did not have that investment to hand. Typically, people who need to do not. The ones that made the investment did so by virtue of their thinking. They chose to be present to the idea of solving a challenge. They were bigger than their problems.

When we close ourselves down because of scarcity our breathing reflects this scarcity by breathing in the chest. This means that when we operate from scarcity we are not present. We are stuck in our own heads.

I urge you to be present. Opportunity is everywhere if only you are present to it. Opportunity also comes to us in the form of a problem to solve. Approaching whatever life throws at you in this way makes you present because your antenna in life is focused outside of you and your own experience. It means your antenna are always looking for solutions.

I will talk to you more about your antenna in the next chapter.

The more people in this world who invest in themselves when they have the chance to, the better a place the world will become. More people who are present to providing value in life will make a bigger difference than many of us believe possible.

My heart has been broken many times by the people who have been unable to invest because of their own scarcity. Then it gets broken again when I meet these people 2 or 3 years later and they are still stuck in the same rut they were when I first met them.

I remember having a friend who, for years, I used to listen to moan and worry about how he never could change and this (awful) experience was always going to happen to him. We lost touch for a good 4 years and then I received a text, out of the blue, saying that he was going to be nearby and would I like to have lunch with him. Yes, said I, keen to find out how life had changed for him in the last 4 years. We met for lunch and he leaped straight back into the same conversation we had had 4 years ago. My heart broke for him yet again.

Invest in yourself, and often. If you can't afford it, change that thinking. Ask yourself how do you afford it instead?

Chapter 2: The 5 Malleable Aspects of Personality

Making a Bigger Difference

*The real focus should be on
contribution; the money will follow*

Where attention goes energy flows. You may have heard the expression, "you can't concentrate on something without concentrating on it".

> "You can have anything you want as long
> as you help enough other people get
> what they want first" – Zig Ziglar

If you would like to dramatically change your fortunes and earn what you are worth, then it is time to make that a no brainer for the people who are paying you.

The people who are paying you look upon you as either a "cost" or an "asset". When they look at you, do they say to themselves "How much..?", or do they say "Wow! What a lot I get from you." If not the second, then how come?

I say this to all of my clients. Focus on providing more value. Find a bigger problem to solve. Make yourself visible by contributing more to the community you are part of. If you focus on the contribution you will find it easier to be present to the opportunity. If you contribute more, then when it is time to consider paying you more, then the bonus is defined by the value they now see in you.

A client of mine, Mina, was working in a large bank in the City of London. She was offered several sideways promotions and had just been offered another one when she and I first met. A sideways promotion is when you are offered a promotion or move that adds no extra pay into your income stream. The bank was using these promotions as an excuse to be seen to be ticking the box in promoting women, and in Mina's case, Asian women. As a result, she had been moved from department to department and, despite the awesome and extremely profitable work she was doing for one particular client (for whom she was the lead), she felt undervalued.

We worked together for 6 months during which we focused on gaining her more visibility and presence. She was constantly told "You talk too fast." We began there, using the breathing exercises like the one at the beginning of this chapter. I will tell you more about that in a later chapter.

The focus of our time together was contributing more. Firstly, we upscaled her network, getting her visibility with more people higher up in the bank. Then we began finding out what they valued, and what they would value more. Once she knew, she set about a plan of making that happen.

She was so successful that the promotion was offered soon after. She was offered a 20% pay rise. With the work we had done together, she had the confidence to say no! She told me she would never have done that without our working together. She came back with "I want 30%" and they immediately said yes. They said yes because it was now a no brainer to pay her at that level. A no brainer because of the value she is now providing at a much higher level.

Where could you be contributing more? What value could you bring to your audience that would give you a 30% pay rise? Or if you run a business, what extra value could you give to your customers that would give you a 30% rise in turnover?

Put your attention here and you will receive more of the attention back you want. Be present to the needs of others, and help them to attain their wants and desires, in order that you attain yours.

The 5 Malleable Aspects of Personality

Most people believe that their personality defines not only who they are, but also what they are capable of. "I'm not the sort of person who…" is a phrase I have often heard people say as a way of making sure they do not try something new.

Much of our personalities are immutable. By that I mean you cannot change that aspect of you.

However, with my clients I look at the 5 areas of personality that social science tells us are malleable. That means that these are areas of potential change for anyone who wants to do something about it.

For instance, is it possible for a person who is retiring and does not like conflict to work on becoming more assertive and transform the way people around them see them? Absolutely, a resounding yes, and often that is a goal that many seek when they come to me.

When I work with my clients, I give them a personality assessment that identifies a score for the 5 malleable areas of personality. Once we have their scores, it will help me to craft and build the coaching intervention that is best likely to help them get their result.

I must acknowledge the work by Professor Jordan Peterson who created the test I use with my clients, "Understand Myself". This is a tool that is invaluable, not because it is infallible, but because the results, whatever they are, always provoke the right conversation for the client, whether they feel it is accurate (which they mainly do) or not (which is when they are triggered by the specifics of a result into looking deeply at that topic). Most of my clients who disagree at first with the result usually look at it again in a couple of months and see the result from a different perspective.

There are two ways of looking at the results from the test. Both are valid approaches.

- One is – this is what you are good at, best stick to that and make sure you are doing more of that.
- The second is – this is what you could be working on, and the evidence tells us that if you work on this that this is the result you will get.

There is also a third way of looking at this – as confirmation that you are working in the right job, or confirmation that you aren't.

However you want to look at these, I thought it might be useful to go through each of the aspects of personality. The test calls these The Big 5, and so I will too.

When you receive the test, it arrives in the form of 100 questions. Your answers will then be compared to the responses of 99 other people in order to gather at what comparable percentile you sit in each of the Big 5.

The mistake that the majority of people think when they receive what they consider a low score, is that the low score means they are bad at something. This is not a good/bad comparable. The score you receive is a "percentile" score rather than a "percentage". The score merely tells you where you sit in relation to 99 other people. Perhaps you might feel you are extremely conscientious and then you get a relatively low score of 30 something and take away that that means you are not very conscientious. Pretty demotivating if you took it that way. Instead, perhaps you might respond to this as, "Huh – I think of myself as pretty conscientious. However, it appears that 60 + people in every 100 are likely to be more conscientious than me. If I want the better results that conscientiousness gives me, that is something to work on."

I hope I have been clear about how this test works and the most useful way that a recipient can respond to it.

Extraversion

*To have more choice in your life you can
train yourself to be more extravert*

This is the first aspect of personality that we look at.

Extraversion can be broken down into 2 areas. These are Enthusiasm and Assertiveness.

Enthusiasm

Enthusiasm is about how much joy there is; Dr Peterson calls it "spontaneous" joy and engagement. Are you in a job, or do you run a company that requires you to have a high degree of joy and engagement with other members of staff, or clients and prospective clients? Do you draw people toward you with your ability to engage with others, or perhaps you might prefer to have a job where you are on your own, preferring that company to the company and energy of others? Perhaps you engage best with data or figures rather than people. Perhaps working online is a better choice for you.

Or perhaps you recognise that if you want to progress into a role higher up the management chain you need to show a level of enthusiasm that attracts that management to want to pay you more. If you do, then you would recognise this is an area for you to work on.

Assertiveness

Assertiveness is about how dominant you are in a social situation. It can typically be measured in vocal terms. How do you dominate a conversation? How likely are you to make sure you are listened to? How likely are people to obey commands quickly if you issue them?

Maybe you work in an environment where this is not a

necessity, again likely because your world does not involve a great deal of social interaction. Maybe you are happy in this environment. A question to ask yourself is around your visibility. Do you have a level of visibility that means people are considering you for moving up in your organisation?

Do you have the desire to be a leader in your field? Do you want to be considered an expert in your particular skill? If so, you will need to develop your assertiveness, because there will be others more assertive in your field who will dominate. When you dominate your field, you are seen and heard and often paid what you are worth.

Conscientiousness

The personality trait most associated with making money

Do I have your attention?

Conscientiousness is the personality aspect that is most associated with earnings and financial wealth. This comes from comparative studies in social science.

I define conscientiousness as the willingness to do that which you do not want to do because your life will be better if you do. For instance, what if you work from home and, after a hectic morning you sit down for lunch, put on the TV and graze in front of a daytime show, designed to be consumed and forgotten within minutes. Or perhaps you find yourself scrolling on Facebook and unable to stop. You know you have at least another 30 telephone calls you should be making this afternoon. On the other hand, there is a guest on your daytime show that you have a vague interest in. "I could do it after this interview is over" goes the voice in your head. "Which voice?" I hear you say. "That voice", I say right back to you.

You wait until the interview is finished then the voice says, "Do it after the show is finished!" The show finishes. The voice in your head says, "Do it later this afternoon!" as you wonder what is coming on TV next. "Do it tomorrow!" says the voice in your head later when you have been in front of the TV for a while. "It won't matter."

Except it does. People with a high conscientiousness score understand that the commodity that is scarce is not money, it is time.

People typically think that time is endless and that there is plenty of it, and that there is only a certain, finite, amount of money in the world. The truth is the other way round. Though time itself is endless, our time on this Earth is not. We are only on this planet for a while, some a shorter time than others.

Money, on the other hand, is an infinite resource. What do governments do when they think there is not enough money in the system? They print some more. When governments do this, it is called "quantitative easing". When ordinary people do this, they go to jail!

The point is resources are there for people to lay their hands on, if their mindset is right.

Time on the other hand is 24 hours a day. Every one of us has the same 24 hours a day. Some make the best use of those 24 hours, and others do not.

You want to make better use of your 24 hours – you want to up your "conscientiousness" score.

Conscientiousness is broken down into 2 areas.

Industriousness is your ability to get through tasks within a specific length of time. Perhaps you are someone who has big lists of tasks at the beginning of the day and you would like nothing better than putting a line of ink through all of the tasks. Perhaps you find you are demotivated by the number of tasks that are still on the list by the end of the day.

Perhaps you are deeply emotionally connected to goal setting and sit in the evening deciding what tomorrow's goals are going to be. What experience do you have at the end of the next day? How often do you accomplish and celebrate because those goals came to pass?

The other aspect of conscientiousness is Orderliness. This is defined by your ability to schedule, organise and create systems that are easy to replicate for yourself.

Life is often a balancing act between the opposing forces of order and chaos. We don't want too much of either in our lives. We often find ourselves walking a fine line. Perhaps our life is too ordered and too predictable? When life is like this, often people sabotage their own lives by bringing in a little chaos in the form of excitement. Perhaps, if a person has a stable marriage and feels their life too ordered, they might find an exciting lover on the side who gives them enthusiasm and pleasure. The trade off is that in exchange for the enthusiasm and pleasure, you take great risks with the rest of your life. If your other half finds out about your lover then the order of your marriage is potentially gone forever.

Perhaps life is too chaotic, and you find it difficult to find order in your life. Perhaps life is so chaotic you find it impossible to set goals and achieve them. Perhaps, if you were that person, you would long for someone to help you find order and simplify your life.

Social science tells us definitively that this is a facet of personality that is the chief signifier of how well someone will do financially. If you want to increase your financial rewards, then this is the game to play, with conscientiousness.

Agreeableness

*How people choose to dismiss
you as a credible force*

Agreeableness is a force that we take into consideration next to conscientiousness. Social science tells us that people who are highly conscientious are likely to be high earners financially. However, if we go into more detail, we find that people with a high level of conscientiousness married to a relatively low level of agreeableness fair much better in life financially, and in terms of professional recognition, than those that have high conscientiousness and high agreeableness. We often find people with those scores end up being used by people with low agreeableness.

Often people with a low agreeableness score see others being more agreeable and use what they see as an excuse to dismiss that person as a force of credibility.

What social science also tells us is that women and men fair differently in results. Perform a test group of 100 women and the average agreeableness percentile is usually 61%. Do a test with 100 men and the average agreeableness score will be approximately 41%.

This means that typically men are less agreeable than women overall and the perception of that agreeableness is why male boards find it so difficult to recognise credibility in the women who seek to be promoted.

This is my specialist area, for most of my clients are women who have sat in the same job for too long and wonder how come less talented men keep being promoted past them.

The important thing is that these men who are doing the dismissing are doing it at an unconscious level. It is the unconscious mind that is getting in the way. I have seen this happen to women in some of the most diversity aware board rooms in the city. At a conscious level they believe they are being fair. In many corporations they insist they run interviews for promotion that are only "competency based". On a conscious level this is true. However, this completely ignores the unconscious mind and the decision making that happens there.

An example is that I work with my clients, so they know how to communicate more assertively and use more direct language. This speaks to the unconscious mind of the listener and as a result, perception of professional credibility increases massively.

Do you remember the story of my client Mina, who worked for one of the world's biggest banks, and who came to me complaining that she was only being offered "sideways" promotions? A sideways promotion means ticking a box. It is a promotion into a different role without any financial rewards. Big banks often do this as a way of ticking the boxes of diversity, especially in appeasing ambitious women without having to offer a reward. Here is a direct word for the big banks who do this. It does not work!

Mina invested in working with my team and I in 2019 and we began work together. We discovered that the perception was "that she could not rise above middle management because she used too many words". We showed her how to be more direct, using shorter sentences, choosing her language carefully, and being willing to be disagreeable whilst communicating up the management chain.

In December 2020, during the pandemic, she was offered a new role and a pay upgrade with the 20% pay rise that I told you about in the previous chapter. If you remember, she now knew how to respond, reject and wait to be paid what she was worth. She called me shortly after she accepted the 30% offer, thanking me, telling me that without our working together on this, she never would have rejected the previous offer.

Maybe, dear reader, Mina's story might resonate with you. Might you want something similar for yourself?

Openness

*Your ability to be open to new
ideas is paramount to growth*

The next personality aspect on our list is Openness. How open are you to hearing ideas that deviate from your accepted beliefs around the world? How easily can you analyse, assimilate and visualise the meaning of new ideas?

Openness is broken down into 2 ideas. "Intellect" and "Openness to Experience".

Openness is really about the ability to be creative. Do you have a creative energy? Do you visualise possibilities then work out plans on how to make those possibilities happen?

The results here can be instructive on whether you are in the right line of work. If you have a high score on "openness to experience" it usually means you crave new experiences and enjoy being out of your comfort zone. One thing is for sure, you won't be happy or fulfilled in a job that requires you to do the same tasks, day in, day out. Often those in the arts – actors, musicians or painters, for instance – will be high in openness to experience.

However, in the corporate space, the strategic thinkers are often high in openness to experience too. They think visually and are responsible for new ideas and the fulfilment of new ideas. If you want to be part of that world, you will be most fulfilled in a senior management position, where the perception is that you are "strategic" rather than "operational" (the 2 terms that often limit the upward movement of many a middle manager) instead of in a middle management position, listening and enacting on other's ideas and instruction.

Intellect is about the ability to absorb ideas and see them in your head. Of course, it feels pretty harsh when a client gets a low score in intellect. For those who mistakenly think it is an assessment of their intelligence. It is not the case.

You can be highly intelligent yet find it difficult to visualise ideas in your mind. Perhaps you lead more with your instincts than your head.

If, for example, you are an entrepreneur, your passion and instinct will help you to establish your business. Unless, however, you have a visualising head you won't be able to grow your business beyond the limits, financially, established by maximising your time. By that I mean, if we assume that the working week is 40 hours (8 hours a day, 5 days a week) then your labour and limits of your labour become the stopping point for your business growth. To go beyond that you have to think strategically, intellectualise new ideas and visualise what putting those ideas into action will look like.

The bottom line regarding this personality aspect is whether you are in the right world of work or not.

Neuroticism

Emotions can destroy your dreams

Nobody likes being called neurotic. I mean, would you?

Here we come to an extremely important part of the assessment. Neuroticism here is used in a clinical sense to mean the emotional response to negative stimuli.

Neuroticism breaks down into 2 different areas of "Withdrawal" and "Volatility".

When one of my clients first came to me, she was stuck in a middle to senior management role in one of the UK's top public sectors. Let us call her Helen. She talked to me of her experience in meetings, finding a lot of her senior management, almost exclusively male and in their late 50s or early 60s, to be frustrating because of their unwillingness to hear her ideas. Her frustration would find its way out in her voice and her energy when she was in the room, and each time it did she would watch as the eyes of her management colleagues around the table would roll up and round as if to collectively articulate "Oh my God, here she goes again!"

Helen's challenge was that she was high in volatility. Faced with a negative emotional experience it was her response to let her emotions out and into the room. When she let her emotions out into the room, then the rest of the room stopped listening.

High levels of emotional volatility are often how people are stopped from advancing. Usually this happens to women, who are typically more attuned to their own emotional experience that most men. The more alpha the male, the less emotional intelligence. This means that these men will find it difficult to identify what emotion is in the room. Yes, they can see that Helen is experiencing an emotion, but "Darned if I know what it is that I am looking at." It is confusing. Since it is confusing, they would rather it was not there. That means the unconscious bias here is not, as many clients believe, men vs women, it is emotions vs logic. Still, it works to the detriment of a lot of women's careers.

There is another woman in that room who is also a client of mine. Volatility is not her issue. Withdrawal is. When she feels negatively about the others in the room and their response to ideas, her habit is to shut down. Withdrawal is the tendency to go quiet when faced with negative emotional stimuli. If you shut down then there can be no chance for visibility.

As a result, my client, Marie Louise, found herself being accused of not being a good leader, because of her lack of visibility. Her office, in the basement of the organisation, meant they put her out of sight and out of mind. Together we had to form a plan for her to go visiting senior stakeholders in the organisation and create the visibility that would change her life. Her visibility improved dramatically outside the organisation where other people started showing more of an interest in her than the management directly above her.

Unfortunately, private companies are unable to offer her an attractive salary that would match that which she is getting within the public sector, so, for us, the search for the right visibility still goes on.

What Is Your Perfect Combination?

Finding the right combination of the Big 5 is the clearest route to making a bigger difference.

This is my challenge for you. After all, I am not you. Therefore I cannot tell you what your perfect combination is. It depends on what your experience is now in the work that you do, and what it is you want to achieve.

Chapter 3: Breathe

JULIET: How art thou out of
breath, when thou hast breath
To say to me that thou art out of breath
– Romeo and Juliet, William Shakespeare

The breath is the basis for everything that happens in your life. Without breath we are dead. Yet many of us never know how to breathe whilst we are alive.

The way human beings breathe defines their experience. Many of us will never know this simple fact and as a result, never change their experience. Most people will go through life never giving their breath consideration. We take it for granted, yet when we are no longer breathing, nothing is possible.

There are 3 different energetic states that any of us can occupy. We move from one of these states to another and to another, constantly shifting moment by moment every day of our lives.

This is the basis of every engagement with any of my clients. The work always begins here.

I'd like you to think of the 3 different states as circles of energy. These circles of energy define how you resonate your energy into the world. Or perhaps your state means you do not resonate energy into the world, but back into yourself.

- The 1st State is the Introvert State.
- The 3rd State is the Convincing State.
- The 2nd State is the State of Presence.

I guarantee that every one of you will, whilst under stress or out of your comfort zone, will revert to either the 1ˢᵗ or 3ʳᵈ state as a default. If you know which is your default, then you can work to undo it and inhabit a state of presence whether you are comfortable or not.

Playing Possum

Making Yourself Invisible means
you have no visibility

The 1ˢᵗ State is the Introvert State. This is circle no. 1.

Do you ever find yourself talking to yourself when you are on your own? Perhaps when you have a problem or a challenge that needs an answer? If that sounds like you, then you are not alone. If you find yourself doing that, you are inhabiting the 1ˢᵗ Circle. The 1ˢᵗ Circle is not a state of presence. After all, if you are having a conversation with yourself, not for the ears of others, why would you need to inhabit a state of presence?

Let us find the 1ˢᵗ Circle. Follow the instruction below. Whilst you are doing so, note your physical response to being in this space. Is it familiar? Is it too familiar?

Stand with your feet hip width apart, parallel under the knees. Move your weight back so you are carrying it on the heel of the foot. Notice what happens to you internally as you do this movement. When you are carrying your weight back of centre, you are in the 1ˢᵗ Circle.

When you lean your weight back, you will find tension tightening in your core. Your centre of gravity is now outside of your body, so your body needs to adapt to stay upright. The tightening means your breath must rise to the chest. Breathing in the chest means breathing more shallowly. It also means breathing more quickly. Your blood will move faster to accommodate this faster breath.

This, in turn, will mean your heart beating faster. Your internal temperature will go up. Your heart, the organ that is in charge of your body, will start sending signals to the hypothalamus. The hypothalamus then steals all the oxygen from the frontal lobe of your brain and holds it at the back. It does this because it interprets the signals from the heart as a sign you are in danger.*

Have you ever had that experience? You are in a meeting and someone is giving you some feedback, perhaps unpleasant, or being delivered in an unpleasant manner. You are thinking, but somehow cannot find the words to respond. Ultimately you stay silent during the process.

The meeting ends and you leave the room. The moment you are in the corridor you suddenly think of 5 or 6 different very clever responses you could have made in the room. Then you admonish yourself for not thinking of it in the room.

The French refer to this as L'Esprit de L'Escalier ('The Spirit of the Staircase'). What I am describing is the experience of being in the 1st Circle whilst under duress and then recovering into a state of presence once your hypothalamus decides you are no longer in danger.

Or perhaps you are at a networking event. You walk in. Nobody knows you. You can see them all looking at you from behind the glass of wine they hold. Panicked by the thought of where to start your body immediately moves back at the overwhelming thought. You then realise that the energy you are giving off is one of "no-one come near me" and everyone is picking up on it.

To end this feeling you turn to your smart phone and start scrolling, in the hope this will signal to the rest of the room how many friends you do have.

---

* I refer you back to chapter 1 where I go into detail about the hypothalamus.

Engaging with your phone is the way a good number of us find we can stay in the 1st circle and therefore miss the great opportunities out in the real world, crossing our paths, never to return.

Do any of these scenarios resonate with you?

Could 1st Circle be your stress default?

Notice how you respond when you are in a stressful situation around work or running a business. Start to check in with your body and breathing when you are faced with news you don't want to hear, feedback you don't like receiving or stress from receiving an email or instruction that makes your life more complicated.

Write notes down and calibrate your body's consistent experience so you can monitor for it again as you work on your confidence and presence.

The Strutting Peacock

When you are convincing, you are not selling

I now refer you to the 3rd Circle. The 3rd Circle of energy is the energy we have when we are forward on the foot. It is the putting on of a show for an audience.

The 3rd Circle is the Convincing Place. It happens when you are overrun by emotion that you have in connection to an outcome.

Perhaps you have an idea that you have worked on for a long time and you feel desperation that this idea should be adopted by your bosses.

Perhaps you have to run a meeting where you must appear to be strong and in charge, but you absolutely don't feel it. You feel the absolute opposite.

Perhaps you feel your job is on the line and the staff you manage absolutely have to do what you tell them to do.

In any of these cases, you might respond with the 3rd circle, the performance of confidence that is not really lived in.

Stand again with your feet hip-width apart, parallel under the knees. Bring your weight forward so you are pitching yourself as far forward as you can, carrying your weight across your toes. Take this as far as you can, without falling over.

Is this familiar?

Notice the internal process when you are in this position. The breath is back in the chest, exactly the same as in the 1st circle. The heart is pumping fast and you can feel your internal temperature rising.

The 3rd Circle is the same experience internally as the 1st circle. It is being reflected out into the world differently.

If you like a simple correlation, this is fight or flight. The 3rd Circle is fight. The 1st Circle is flight. With the 3rd Circle you square up your body far forward in preparation for combat. In the 1st Circle you make your body as small as possible in order that you appear invisible to potential opponents.

Check this out for yourself. Try moving from the 1st through to the 3rd circle positions. Notice your internal experiences at the 2 extremes. Notice first your internal process. The heart. The breath. The tensions you hold in your body. Notice what is the same. Notice what is different.

Write your notes down. The more you are aware of your internal processes the more the chance you will change your experience of life. Writing this down begins your intellectual process of shifting into a new way of being.

How much did you resonate with the experiences I note above about a person in 3rd Circle?

For everyone who is reading this book, 1st or 3rd will be a stress default. Maybe both. Which do you believe is yours?

Being Grounded

When you are grounded people can feel it

The eagle eyed among you will have noticed that I skipped from 1st circle to 3rd.

Absolutely correct. It was intentional.

I am now coming to the 2nd Circle. The 2nd circle is the position of presence.

When you are in either 1st or 3rd, you cannot have presence for others. For a start, you have none of your frontal lobe available to use. No oxygen. The oxygen is all stored at the back of the brain ready to arm your muscles for that dash to get away from the sabre-toothed tiger. Thinking is a huge effort, so all your energy is co-ordinated behind being internally focused. You have no energy for the outside world, so how can the outside world have energy for you?

You may recognise that there are times in your life when you are in flow. You flow through tasks and connections naturally and people and opportunities flow to you, naturally. Whilst you are feeling this you are in the 2nd circle, the position of presence. You are present in yourself. You have presence for others.

This means that you have to find a way to be present in yourself. Without it you cannot have presence for others.

Have I got your curiosity yet? Would you like to know how to achieve this?

Stand again with your feet hip-width apart, parallel under the knees. This time you carry your weight centrally, perhaps slightly forward so the weight is just a little on the balls of the feet.

Now your centre of gravity is inside you. There is no danger of you falling over. When we have tried the previous circles your centre of gravity was outside the body.

With the centre of gravity inside you the breath easily

drops down into the stomach. Now you are breathing into the stomach, you are breathing lower and slower. With this slower breath, your heart rate lowers too. The heart stops sending signals to the brain telling it there is danger. The hypothalamus releases all the oxygen back into the frontal lobe of the brain. With all this extra oxygen your experience of life changes dramatically. You feel calmer, more confident. You become more flexible physically.

Stay with this for a moment and feel which muscles are working when the breath is in the stomach. Ideally you feel your abdominal muscles working. The muscles that are in the 'v' of the groin area are moving, open and closed as you take that breath deep. How does taking your breath this deep change your experience of the world?

Now maybe you are finding it tricky to get your breath as low as I am describing. Perhaps you would like to know an exercise, a life hack, that you can use to find this experience instantly, especially during those moments when you might be tempted to go back into 1ˢᵗ or 3ʳᵈ, your chosen stress default.

When you do this next exercise take good care to look after yourself. You, after all, are in your own world as you read this. I advise you do this exercise when you are on your own and in a safe environment to play. If you did this in a crowded office, it would certainly get you visibility, maybe not the visibility you want.

Stand again in the now familiar position of feet hip-width apart, parallel under the knees. Close your eyes and come up onto your toes. This should make you feel off balance.*

---

* We remove the eyesight from the equation in order to give the other senses the chance to wake up and serve you. Eyesight is the sense we trust the most to give us information about the world. Eyesight lies to us. There is so much information that eyesight has to delete and interpret things for us in order to cope. Sometimes, the way eyesight does this is not helpful to us in achieving our desires. I advocate the use of all senses. I had a client at one of

Roll your weight across your feet, from toes to ball to heel and then back again so you are rocking between the 3 circle energies. Keep this up for at least a minute, keeping the eyes closed at all times. The braver you are at extending this the more you will feel off balance. This is why I suggest doing this in a safe space. You want to make sure if you trip or lose balance completely, there is no danger to you.

After one full minute, with your body fully off balance, we will start to come back to standing. The important piece here is to keep your eyes closed as you do. Keeping you off balance with eyes closed will have turned up the volume on your other senses. They will now come into play to help you "feel" when you are back in balance. This means, your awareness now being inside you rather than outside in the world, that you will feel the moment the breath drops into the stomach and note where you are carrying your weight as you do so.

Now you are in balance, breath dropped into the stomach, and you are standing still with your eyes closed. Keep them closed, calibrate your body, and place your head where you feel that you are looking directly ahead of you. When you feel your head is looking directly ahead of you, then, and only then, open your eyes.

Is this eyeline you have now higher or lower than your everyday eyeline?

For many of my clients this is a revelation. So many of the

---

the biggest banks in the UK. He was financial director there. I had started work with him whilst he was with another large bank. When he left the previous bank, they had to employ 2 people to do his job, so hard did he work. His nickname at the new bank was "Bull in a China Shop". When he came to me whilst in the new role (more stressful than even the last) his head was hunched down, his shoulders raised, and his body pushed forward as if he was about to charge me. Exactly like a bull expecting trouble. When I asked him to stand straight and look directly ahead of him, he said "I am!". Doing the above exercise was a revelation for him. He found behavioural flexibility through it and changed the relationship he had with his finance team.

women I work with find the experience of looking directly ahead of themselves a new and vibrant one. They have spent so much time in the 1st circle.

If your eyeline is higher than usual, it suggests that your stress default is 1st Circle.

If your eyeline is lower than usual, it suggests that your stress default is 3rd Circle.

It is not an exact science and some of you will find you have experience of both. However, what you find is highly likely to be the main place you go to in time of stress.

Some of you may find no change at all. Excellent. That suggest you might be used to finding this 2nd circle for yourself already.

Again, note down your answers.

Do this exercise every day for a period of 30 days. Tell your body this is your new way of breathing. Tell your body this is your new way of standing.

Your Connection With the World

Place your antenna out into the
world, not inside your own head.

I am going to assume that you can now find your 2nd circle position using the exercise above.

This chapter is about so much more than your own individual experience. It's true that your individual experience resonates out into the world and influences the energies of others. This is what I mean by "You have to be present in yourself in order to have presence for others."

Do the rocking exercise again.

Once you come back to standing you notice your own experience, physical, mental and emotional.

Now let's take your attention to the outside world. What can you feel in the space you are in?

Many people find they are aware of many more things when they are in the 2nd circle. After all, your brain is now flooded with oxygen, so you have much more brain power than the basics you have in 1st or 3rd.

Perhaps you might hear a clock ticking. Perhaps you might hear birds chirping outside your window. Perhaps you can now hear the hum of electrical devices in the room with you. Many clients describe a heightened awareness of sound.

Or perhaps your awareness of smell develops. Immediately you are in the 2nd circle space the sense of smell develops. Perhaps you are tempted to open a window. Perhaps you are aware of the scent of candles or air freshener.

What if you ate a meal in the 2nd circle? How might your experience of the food and drink change because you are now present to it? Maybe you already know the difference between sitting down to concentrate on the experience of a meal. Maybe you can tell the difference when you eat whilst watching the television, or trying to concentrate on your phone.

The one that surprises my clients the most is the awareness of others in a room or a space. Without looking they discover they have a new and heightened awareness of the placement of others. This realisation, often new because they have spent the majority of their lives in 1st, or occasionally 3rd, is the first step to understanding the possibilities of their influence in the world, beyond just what they see and hear.

Start exploring this for yourself. As suggested above, do the rocking exercise every day for 30 days and see what you start to notice for yourself. How are you resonating further? What are you aware of that you were not before? Where could you use this to your advantage in the world you are part of? Who would benefit if you did resonate further in the world?

Imagine what might be possible if you are speaking to an audience whose behaviour you would like to influence? If you had your antenna out there in the audience, awareness of their experience and the physical flexibility to respond to it, what might be possible for you?

Taming Your Fears

Your physical experience defines your
mental and emotional experience

The only thing that is worse than the fear of taking action, is the regret you experience when you don't.

Now you should be able to feel the difference in experience in the 3 Circles and the value of being in the 2nd as your default state for life. Therefore I have recommended twice in this chapter that you do the rocking exercise once a day over a period of 30 days.

I want my clients to be able to perform their duties, presentations and conversations without having to put any thought toward anything we are discussing here. Working in isolation whilst you are safe from risk, means you are gaining the confidence to eventually take these skills into a world where there may be some small risk, and following success with that, the big risks.

Every human being experiences fear at some point. I remind you of the story I told at the beginning of the book about the American football player for whom "fear is not in his vocabulary". If that were true of you, it would be one of the least wise places to be. Sometimes fear is to be respected, sometimes it is there for us to jump over.

In order to jump over fear, we must harness confidence. The first step to doing that is to liberate the body from the physical impact of that fear. We must make sure fear has no purchase on our ability of function physically in the world.

Think of an action you want to take, but it scares you to do it. Notice what happens to your breathing when you consider the idea of doing this. What is the worst that can happen? See it in your mind's eye. Your brain can't tell the difference between what you imagine, and that which is true. Let that brain go to work and calibrate your body.

The breath rises into the chest.

Where else can you feel tightness? Which muscles are hardening and getting tight in your body? Is there a tightness in your chest? Does your face go red as you undergo this experience? Are you afraid others can see this?

Now we are aware of this, let's undo it. The key is in your breath. We are working from the outside in. When we adjust our breath, you will see the world as it is, not worse, not better.

It is time for the rocking exercise. Do the rocking exercise. Come back to standing. Find that space where you are looking directly ahead of you. Remember what it feels like to hold your eyeline down, like you may have done when fearful. Notice how you are breathing now. Focus on the breathing into the stomach. Give your attention to the muscles in the v of the groin. Feel them opening and closing to help the air get as low as you can. Slow that heart rate down by focusing on the breath.

If you find this difficult, then focus on the big toe of the right foot. Isolate it, give it your attention and then press it gently into the ground. This should force a big in-breath right down into the stomach. Once, many years ago, I had the whole of the board of Coutts Bank repeating the mantra in their heads "Big toe right foot" as a way of clearing their minds before having a board meeting.

Now visualise again the action that you were fearful of.

How are things different now? What has changed in your experience? What do you see as the possibilities of taking this action? Do you now feel you can step over this fear and DO it?

Write it all down. Do it with a pen and paper. Not on a screen. Bring your body into the process. Connect your body to your mind. Operate as one unit, aware of all components.

Making Others Feel Safe

*People follow the breath pattern of the
most certain person in the room*

You have it in your power to affect the experience of many others. Your physical behaviour can make an audience, large or small, members of your family, the board or people you meet every day in your life. You have the power to make them feel safe and secure in your company, and in your skills.

You do this with your breath.

Remember I said this in the first chapter. Forgive me repeating this. However, I do know that spaced repetition of ideas and exercises creates real change for people, so I make no apology.

Leadership is not about exercising power over others. History has, and always will, show us that those who try to lead this way may have a small amount of time when they have leadership. It never ends well for them. Hitler and Mussolini may have had power over most of Europe in 1939, but they had lost all of it and their lives too by 1945. This should be a lesson for all who fail to understand what history is trying to tell us.

Good leadership and long-term leadership come from consent. The group who you lead must trust you to allow you to lead effectively.

We must satisfy the unconscious minds of our staff. The way we do this is through the breath. This is the best method of creating rapport with people who are different to you.

When you lead a group they will adopt your breath pattern. If you lead the group in either the 1st circle (with timidity or uncertainty) or the 3rd circle (with a false confidence you are faking) the unconscious mind of your group will know because they will adopt your breath pattern and feel exactly as you do. If you are fearful, they will be too. This means that whatever task you have in mind for them, they will be fearful as they do it. They will take your fear out of the room with them.

On the other hand, if you lead with certainty, breathe with certainty, from the 2nd circle position, your audience will take your certainty and confidence, as they will breathe with your breath pattern, in the room and as they leave and take on the task.

The influence of breath on the lives of others is immeasurable. This is a super skill and it affords you the courage to find more super skills and make them yours.

Write down what super skills you would like to have now that you have spent time with the 2nd circle.

The breath absolutely needs to be in place before we can access the powerful voice you have and have not yet accessed.

In the next chapter we will look in depth at the possibilities for you in nurturing the most ill-used asset that every human with a voice box has. Before we can do this, acquaint yourself with the 3 circles and use the rocking exercise to make the 2nd circle your daily default.

Chapter 4: Voice

The 3 Voices

*You naturally have a huge range, you
just don't know how to use it*

We are all born with a powerful voice. That is all of us who are born with a voice box in the throat area.

Many people believe they have a "quiet voice" or their voice is not very loud, or does not travel far. If you have ever said that of yourself, recognise that it is simply not true.

Many women have often been told their voice isn't very loud by men who they work with. It is really an excuse, from those men, for treading on the women in the room when they are speaking. This information comes from a recent Harvard University study listing women's experience in the board-room and male experiences of women in the boardroom. It's extraordinary to see how much of the commentary on both sides of the fence focuses on the voice, the experience of making a voice heard and the experience of being heard, or not being able to hear a voice.

We know that 38% of creating a first impression in a room is based on the experience of the voice.

If you are reading this and saying to yourself, "Damn it, David, I am one of those people. I DO have a quiet voice. How dare you say I don't!" then I totally get why you might think that.

Instead of "having" a quiet voice, I'd like you to think of it like this. You are "using" a quiet voice.

We are all born with a powerful voice.

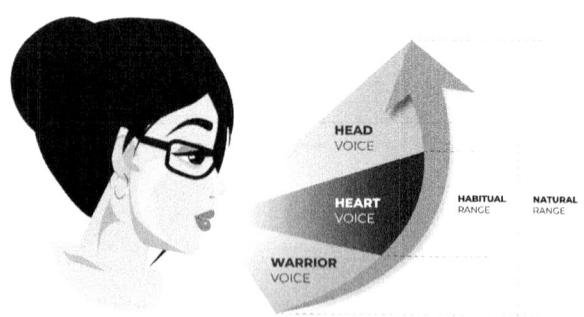

We are all born with a huge range. We scream our way out into the world (and are often rewarded by a Doctor or Midwife by a smack on the bottom (what a great way to enter the world!)). Gradually throughout our childhood, we learn to use less and less of the range in our voice. This is often helped along by adult ideas about conforming and the virtue of being silent. If you, whilst you were being brought up, were ever subject to ideas like "children should be seen and not heard" then perhaps you understand. In the first 7 years of life we are downloading into our brains constantly everything that our parents and primary carers say to us. We do this in order to learn the important skill of functioning within the social structures created around us. After all, like the caveperson of old, if we stand out too much, there is a danger of rejection and rejection means hunger, cold and death.

By the time most of us are 18 years old we are using a fraction of the range that naturally has been given to us. We don't, typically, know how to use our voice powerfully any more. That is when we start telling ourselves stories about our voice. To be direct, it is an excuse for letting ourselves not be heard.

Stretch your arms in the air, as far apart as you can stretch. Hold one hand as high above your head as you can. Hold the other as low as you can. Chart the distance between your hands in your mind.

Imagine this distance is your vocal range. The hand above your head is the highest note in your voice. The lower hand, the lowest notes in your voice. We call this your natural range.

Now, without thinking, move your hands closer together so the distance reflects the range you believe you use in your voice. For most of you this new range will be approximately a 3rd of the previous natural range. We call this your habitual range. This is the range you have learned to use out of habit.

Would you like to know how to extend the habitual range, so it is more like your natural range?

Assuming that is a "Yes!" read on.

As a voice specialist, I break down the natural range of the voice into 3 different areas which have specific resonance to the listener.

In an ideal world we all want to have equal access to all 3 of the voices, naturally, and without thinking about it. Let's start by examining what the 3 Voices are. It is up to you to decide which of the 3 is the one you need to develop first.

Being More Credible

*The perception of credibility is
transferred through the Warrior Tone*

The first voice we are looking at is the Warrior Voice.

The Warrior Voice consists of the lowest notes in the voice. The Warrior Voice is where men love to resonate, especially when they are together and forming domination hierarchies. Forming domination hierarchies is normal for men. Women do it too, with each other, only women do it differently. We are talking about Alpha dominance here. Every time a group of men are together in a room they will sort themselves out in a dominance hierarchy. They will do this unconsciously. I have sat in the most "diverse" and "inclusive" boardrooms where the men have every intention on a conscious level to be open and inclusive. However, unconsciously, they are still in competition with each other to form the hierarchy. Men form hierarchies over anything where they feel they can be judged in relation to other men. This could be anything from sports, performance in a sales role, contribution in a boardroom, or performance on a video game. Often men who consider themselves to be "nerdy" and therefore not competitive are running deep seated domination dynamics with other gamers they play against.

One of the ways that men form these hierarchies is through who has the lowest tone of voice. Listen to a group of men in a bar automatically resolving themselves in their hierarchy. At an unconscious level men associate low tone of voice to high levels of competence and credibility.

Men don't, naturally, run dominance hierarchies with women. After all, at the most basic level, the reason men create these hierarchies is for the benefit of the women in the room.

Traditionally, up until the 1960s, women avoided using the warrior voice for fear of being considered "masculine". When women started becoming successful in the boardroom they found they had to embrace being more masculine, in order to compete with the boys in the room.

Margaret Thatcher was the first British premiere to work with a voice coach to, deliberately, lower her voice and be the warrior for the benefit of her all-male cabinet. When she entered Downing Street as Prime Minister in 1979 she was operating in the Heart Voice (which I will get to soon). She was one of the 3% of women who made up Parliament. She led an entirely male cabinet who soon proved themselves out of control. Her popularity was waning. An election was coming soon. She turned to a voice coach, Gordon Reece, and to the first lord of the British theatre, Laurence Olivier, to help her embrace the warrior voice. This voice is what lead to the Soviets dubbing her

The Iron Lady. This voice and the iron resolve she portrayed helped her seal the election victory as well as winning the war against the Argentinians over the Falkland Islands. If you want an example of this please seek out the 2 video clips on You Tube, the first showing that first day she moved into Downing Street and then the more famous "The Lady is Not For Turning" speech. These voices are worlds apart.

Whatever you may think of Margaret Thatcher's politics, you surely respect that the vocal change creates a different impression and left the British people (who voted for her) feeling that hers were the safest hands to leave the country in.

By contrast, Neil Kinnock was considered a great orator (better than Thatcher) and could bring great emotional experience into his speeches. He displayed passion beautifully. However, he left the majority of people feeling he was not the right person to run the country.*

In the 21st Century we are looking at a different kind of female leader. Women don't want to be successful by emulating the behaviours of men. They want to create their own identity and style. Sometimes a client can be resistant, at first, to the idea of the warrior voice. I respect that resistance. I do let them know that the warrior voice has power as one of the tools any of you might use to create a higher credibility perception in your work.

Margaret Thatcher's Warrior Voice worked for her in the short term, but long term it was a disaster. She was stabbed in the back by her competition and replaced by John Major whilst still in office. This was because she lacked flexibility. Her warrior voice, by now, was all she was displaying. It made her look like a woman full of hubris. It left the impression that she listened to no-one.

---

* I raise this point because it is important to understand that you can be a brilliant speaker and it will have no impact unless you are speaking directly to the unconscious minds of your audience. Consider what your audience needs at that level when you create anything they need to hear.

That is why, earlier in this chapter, I advised anyone to develop all 3 voices, so you have flexibility to work with. It will make it easier to be heard as a well-rounded leader (or emergent leader).

Being More Approachable

Rapport is created at an unconscious level

Now we move to the Heart Voice.

- The Heart Voice is the centre of the voice.
- Think of the Warrior Voice as being the voice of information delivery.
- Think of the Heart Voice at the voice of seeking information.

The Heart Voice is how we display empathy. This is how we build rapport with others. It is the voice we would use when we are asking questions. Perhaps you might want someone to feel welcome and safe in your company. Perhaps you might like people to perceive you as an equal.

Tonally we are much softer when we are in the Heart Voice. If you are a manager who wants to make their staff feel safe to come to you when there is a problem, then you would use the heart voice when you tell them that "My door is always open". If you attempted that in Warrior, I guarantee that no one will ever seek your help and problems would be secreted until they become problems for you as well as your team.

Typically women are more comfortable here. After all, women are more likely to be interested in fairness and the idea of fair distribution. A female leader is more likely to use "soft power" to get the buy-in of her team. Any leader who uses these tones, authentically, will command huge levels of respect and loyalty in their team. I've seen this work very well when clients have come to me wanting to get their team engaged in a way as never before to deliver as a unit and create results the company has never seen. If you want to create behaviour change in your staff, this tool of soft power will be an essential part of your kit.

When I work with men they often have the credibility piece off pat using their warrior voice and are completely unaware of the emotional engagement of the staff they lead. As women have traditionally avoided being seen as "masculine" by not using the warrior voice, men will avoid the higher notes of the heart voice for fear of being seen as "emotional".

The sad truth, for any of my male readership, is that the emotional experience of your staff is paramount to the results that any team creates. Ignore this at your peril.

The great leaders have emotional flexibility. The great leaders have vocal flexibility. They are always in the 2nd circle, their antenna out there among their people, listening and feeling what is happening in a room. People signal their needs through the tonality of their voice. They signal through their own choice of tone as to what they need from you at that particular moment.

Think back to the leaders you have been influenced by. What tones did they use? How flexible were they, tonally and emotionally?

Listen to Barack Obama's speeches. Particularly the speech he performed at least 8 times during his first Presidential campaign. It was so popular that it was brought out of retirement and played (like a favourite old movie) as the last speech of his 2nd Presidential campaign. On You Tube you will find this under the search term "All Fired Up". Listen to how his voice moves from warrior to heart and back to warrior. I can assure you he no longer needs to think about any of this whilst he is performing. The effect on his audience is remarkable. Using the Heart Voice he weaves a tale that resonates deeply with that audience and they elect him through that amazing skill.

I come back to the Obama story to remind you that when my mentor Patsy Rodenburg met him he was described as a man with "no presence and no charisma". I remind you because any one of you is capable of the impact and massive influences that he created in his campaign toward a goal he wanted.

Being More Enthusiastic

Enthusiastic leadership wins the day

Now we head up to the Head Voice, the final of the 3 Voices.

- The Head Voice is the highest of the notes we can do.
- The Head Voice is the voice of enthusiasm.
- The Head Voice is the voice of high emotions.

This may sound like something we have already talked about in the Heart Voice piece. The Head Voice is to be used sparingly and in specific situations.

The Head Voice is best deployed when you are speaking to groups. If you attempted this on a one to one, they might run from the room. After all, the highest notes can feel harsh, too harsh for a one-to-one conversation.

The Head Voice brings BIG emotions into a room. Its value is in getting the group to buy-in to an idea. Perhaps you might need your team to work late, later than they might want to. Perhaps on a Friday. You might want to build up buy-in to the idea that "we can all pull together, burn the midnight oil, get this down and done before the deadline". You might want to promise a reward. "Let's do this! I will buy the pizza for every-one." If you do this, you want emotional buy-in for that reward.

The Head Voice is best used managing down the chain rather than up. If you want to impress those who are above you in the chain, stick to the warrior voice and bring the heart in after your first impression has been successful.

Typically both men and women avoid these higher registers. Men do this because of the extremity of emotional connection to these notes. Women, because they don't want to be judged for the perception they fear these notes will leave.

It is a mistake to ignore the power of using the head voice in a judicious way. It is always worth warming up these notes as part of your tool kit.

Those are the 3 voices and their value in the workplace you occupy. Now is the time to work out where you want to start. What is the voice you are not using and most need to have access to? What will give you the quickest reward in the way others perceive you?

Warming Up the Voice

Your voice is a musical instrument
to be treated with care

I imagine you are wondering what to do to activate one or more of these voices in your own.

Here we are.

Your voice is a musical instrument and needs to be treated with care. There are certain tones that, if you are not properly warmed up, or breathing from the stomach, will damage the vocal chords. The vocal chords are a muscle. Like all muscles they can bruise and tear. The most likely cause of bruising is breathing from the chest, when the breath is too close to the chord, which is too harsh and causes bruising. You cannot bruise your vocal folds with breath from the stomach.

Firstly, make sure you have done your exercises from the previous chapter. I shall now assume you are able to find and are in the 2nd circle. If you are struggling with that, may I suggest you go back and find a solution before you attempt to warm up your voice?

Treat the voice gently.

We start with humming. A gentle hum. Put your lips together, take a breath down into the stomach and hum as you breathe out. Now this hum, the noise you make right now, is likely to be the centre of your habitual voice. Note where you think it might sit in your natural range. Perhaps lower than centre, perhaps higher.

Are you comfortable that the hum you are making now is supported by the muscles deep in the abdomen? When you hum does it sound secure or wobbly. If wobbly, focus on your breathing. Give your attention to the muscles in the v of the groin. Once focused, does this sound more secure?

Once this note is secure we can move onto making other notes happen.

It's your choice now. Do you want to try a higher or a lower note first? Go for it! Deep breath in, and hum. Once this is secure try a note at the other end of the spectrum.

You have a huge natural range and a smaller habitual range. That means some of the notes will come easily and some not so easily. Just like any other tool, we will apply a little oil to the notes that do not come so easily. The oil we apply is still water. Please don't drink juice or carbonated water when you are warming your voice up. Both of these drinks dry the vocal folds out, and fruit juice, being acidic in nature, will actively expand the vocal folds, meaning there is less space between them to make sound. Still water is the only oil that helps the voice to work.

The other oil we apply is the hum itself. The humming I ask of you here is gentle and should never be forced. Be gently persistent with the notes that are tricky to make, drink water, be persistent again. Soon these vocal folds will understand you want them to work now and they will come to your aid.

Spend the next 5 minutes humming different notes in your range. Try high, then low, then high again. Wander as you do this. Perhaps perform a menial task whilst you hum. Test as many notes as you can in this time. Give time to the one's that feel less secure over the ones that do. Test the extremities of high and low. No need to be concerned if a note is tricky to sustain. Give it a little more time, lubricate with still water and try again.

Once this is done you are ready for the exercises that will help you develop the 3 Voices.

How to Practice

Do these exercises daily for 4 to 6 weeks and people will respond to you completely differently

Now is the time to get practical.

I am going to assume you have done your humming exercises and warmed up the vocal chords. If you haven't, then do so before you attempt the exercises below.

You will need to find a space to work in, where you can stretch your arms out in front and back of you without hitting something (or someone).

The Warrior Voice

- Start with your feet hip-width apart, parallel underneath the knees.
- Plant one foot forward and the other behind and lower your centre of gravity, gently bouncing so it might look as if you were pretending to ride a horse. Make this a stretch, but not a stretch that is so uncomfortable that it is difficult to keep up, or that you feel you might fall over.
- Place one hand on the stomach in the shape of a fist. Place the other on the lower back, also in the shape of a fist.

- Start feeling the breath in your stomach against the 2 hands.
- Take a deep breath into the stomach and as you exhale you will exclaim out loud "Aha!" whilst at the same time extending both hands out in a stretch, maintaining the fist, as if you were firing that "Aha!" out as far as it can go.
- The "Aha!" noise you make will activate the Warrior inside you.

Many of my clients have felt shocked at the resonance and depth of what they can create using this exercise.

Do this exercise at least twice and then start speaking. The voice does not need a lot of practice to start working properly for you. Most of those vocal muscles have been dormant for a long time. Using this exercise you will wake them up and make them go to work for you.

Start speaking now and notice how your voice sounds as you speak. Lower notes coming out? Good.

The Heart Voice

- To activate the heart voice we begin with our feet hip-width apart, parallel under the knees.
- Place your hands on your shoulder blade. As you do this you will find the rib cage is opening with the breath. This is how we get the higher notes of the heart voice moving.
- Take a breath in and as you exhale exclaim "Aha!" whilst extending your arms high above your head, and out in an ellipse curved shape.
- You will find the note you are making is higher and the voice you speak in will be too.

Those of you who are aware of British comedy may recognise this sound and movement from the early career of Steve

Coogan's character Alan Partridge. In his early BBC chat show "Knowing Me, Knowing You" he entered the stage doing this movement and sound. There will be videos of this on You Tube if you are tempted to look. For those of you who are familiar with this, you may find yourself laughing as you do this exercise, which is totally fine by me. The laugh may even help loosen up tension and make the exercise even more effective.

The Head Voice

Let us get enthusiastic.

- Stand in the usual way, feet hip-width apart, parallel under the knees. Get used to this being your starting position.
- Place your fingers on the temples of your skull. Notice how much more the rib cage is extending as you do this.
- Deep breath in. As you exhale you will make the sound "Ping!" and your arms will fire up in an arc as far as they can go. This will access the highest notes in your register.

Remember that the Head Voice has value in certain situations and none in others. I have described these situations in the chapter above. It would be a mistake to miss out on making sure that the head voice is available to you.

***

Now you know more about how the voice works, how in the voice world we break the voice down into 3 specific areas that have specific resonance for those listening. You also have a number of exercises to warm up the voice and work on developing the areas of the voice you feel you need to have access to in order to create the impact and impression you want people to have.

As we finish the chapter I have questions for you. They are questions for you to ask yourself. Find a piece of paper and something to write with. You will want to refer back to these as you are defining the future you want to create.

- What do I need more of in my role? – Credibility/Rapport/Enthusiasm
- What I am going to do with this now I know it? Only action changes things.
- Write down 3 "Ahas!" you had whilst reading this chapter.
- Where can I use this? Think specifically about the conversations, meetings and opportunities to make quick wins happen for you by deploying these techniques.

It takes 4 to 6 weeks of little but often practice to change a voice and change perception with that voice. To make that happen, you have to be committed to taking action. That means every day, 5–10 minutes of humming and doing the exercises out loud.

Sometimes people hear this new voice coming out of their mouths and think "That's not me!" I remember one client saying to me, "I can't take this voice back home to my husband. He won't recognise me." To any client who feels that way I would like to make it clear that the noise coming out of your mouth at any time is your voice. These are your vocal chords, no one else's. If you are fearful of someone else in your life hearing your new voice, ask yourself "how come?". What is it you are afraid of them thinking or feeling about hearing this new voice?

"Anything we want is on the other side of fear." This quote from Jack Canfield is an absolute truth. If we hear our own voices and become fearful, ask yourself what it is you are really scared of. It's likely to be rejection or judgement. Those are the 2 fears most of us need to step over in order to make a greater difference in the world.

Chapter 5: Energy

More energy – more success

*Millionaires all have more energy
than those around them*

Something that has been self evident from the time I spend around successful people is that they have more energy than most others.

Those who make things happen in the world have the same 24 hours as the rest of us. Yet they use that 24 hours with a different energy to the rest of humanity.

Often it is how you enter the world every morning when you wake that defines the energy that you have the rest of the day.

Many people struggle to find the energy to do the most mundane tasks daily. Others find that they start the day early with a drive and a passion running through the blood in their veins and the muscles in their bodies, meaning they attack the day, accomplish, celebrate their accomplishments, and go to bed satisfied and sated, ready to make the best of sleep.

Where do you believe you sit?

For many years I sat in the former camp. I trained as an actor and hung out with other, less successful, actors from my years at drama school. Energetically, poor actors are not the best community to be part of and that was reflected in the results I created in my world. I did achieve work, and I did enjoy tremendously (and was seriously energised when I did have work) the times I was working as either actor or director. Many days were spent unenergized between jobs. In that time I did little for myself to move my life forward in a significant way.

This would also be true of many of my colleagues. We would get together over coffee and cake (my emotional drug of choice) to commiserate and validate the experiences we were having, and justify our decisions not to change our lives.

One day my dear sister dragged me along to a personal development seminar by Tony Robbins. It was staggering how much energy that man has. He opened the day at 9am and didn't leave the stage until 5pm. (I know that he has delivered his seminars for between 15 and 20 hours without leaving the stage to eat or visit the loo.) He is powered by love, love for all of us in his audience. In the audience with me that day were 7000 people. He had to bring a lot of love for everyone in that space, and my goodness, I had never seen or felt anything like it.

This thought lodged in my mind and I decided I was going to take positive action to change my life. For myself and for my family.

Mind you, even though I had all the resources I needed within myself, it took a little while to percolate into my mind and body. I created a system to help my clients have access to the energy they needed to shine and make a bigger difference in their worlds. It took a while to realise that I needed to listen to my own advice.

3 years ago I was diagnosed with Diabetes Type 2. It was a shock to me when it was revealed, and I went through the usual stages of grief upon finding out.

"My body has let me down" went the voice in my head. When I articulated it out loud to one of my business mentors he said to me, "Perhaps you should rethink that. What if it turned out you had let your body down?"

That was the truth I didn't want to hear. I rejected it at first. After 24 hours I embraced that truth and since then the mornings have changed dramatically. I now had something that was an absolute "must" to get me out of bed; exercising first thing and transforming my experience of the day.

I ended up using my own techniques much more than I had prior to the diagnosis.

Last year, my blood reading was below the scale of what is considered as having Diabetes. I am now officially in remission.

The morning routine stays.

In this chapter I will show you some of the techniques I use with my clients that makes immediate results happen. Change of perception is instantaneous when using these. Some are for long-term use, some for what my clients term "just in time" use, immediately before you enter the meeting.

Engaging the Whole Body

*This is to maximise your immediate ability
to create emotion and value in a room*

Have you ever had that experience that menial tasks, or things you can usually do easily, become tasks that feel like wading through treacle?

I think this is quite a normal human reaction to waking up in the morning for many of us. After all, the change of state between unconscious and conscious is huge and the movement from having no awareness of your body's state to immediate, visceral awareness of your body's state can be a shock.

Have you ever woken up and wanted to pull the covers over you head and go back to sleep? Be honest, I know I have many times through my life.

Connecting the mind and the body for action is the key to getting past that stage of waking up.

Have you ever looked at the clock knowing you have an

important meeting in 5 minutes and think to yourself, "If only I had more time to be ready for this"?

I banished those feelings and thoughts through the exercises I am sharing in this chapter.

Here is the first of these exercises.

- Stand in the usual position, feet parallel under the knees. Make sure you have space around you for this exercise. Have a clear path immediately around you in all areas.
- Lift one hand out in front of you, holding it outstretched.
- Shake your hand. Shake it hard. Shake it fast. Shake your hand until you feel tingling in the fingers.
- Now extend the shaking into the forearm. Move that forearm around in a circle fast. Feel the blood moving fast as you extend this shaking. Give this another 20 seconds before extending it to the whole arm.
- Let the entire arm go crazy. As if the arm was not yours and it is whipping about, out front, to the side, behind like a separate entity to the rest of you.
- Now that you have that feeling, that your arm is a separate entity to you, engage with this idea. You want rid of that arm! Find the nearest window and throw that arm away from you as if you wanted it to go through the window. Do this at least 3 times before stopping and letting the arm hang by your side.
- What do you feel now?

Usually, my clients feel energised on one half of their body. The blood is moving more freely, and they have an awareness of the extremity of their fingertips.

It also usually leaves them feeling lopsided. They also look lopsided with the arm they have worked on looking longer than the other. It is longer, because the exercise has loosened tension held in the joints, the wrist, elbow and shoulder.

So repeat the same exercise with the other hand and arm.

How do you feel after doing both arms?

Many of my clients feel exhilarated and animated. They rediscover their flexibility and strength to take on whatever task they have been fearful of approaching.

I recommend this exercise for the 5 minutes before that difficult meeting, before ringing that client you have been avoiding and for the moment where you feel you are just not up to it.

If you are feeling adventurous, you might want to do the same exercise with your feet and legs. Start by circling the foot from the ankle and then giving it a shake. Then move up to moving the bottom half of the leg about, then shaking the whole leg before trying to "get rid of it" by throwing it out of the window. Don't forget to do both legs if you want to do this exercise.

The Bunny Hop

This one little trick is a life hack
for maximum energy

Fear of embarrassment is often the thing that stops us from taking a step outside the norm.

Experience has told me, all the way back to my days working in the theatre, that the spoils go to the people willing to be unreasonable. Unreasonable as defined is willing to do what the majority would not. The majority are too agreeable and fearful of a negative response to risk taking real action, to be seen and heard as a leader.

So here is a test. It is a life hack for those who have done the exercise above and are ready for a quick hack.

It is called The Speak to Shine Bunny Hop.

- You are going to pretend to be a bunny. Silly, right.

Great that it is silly too. We often take ourselves far too seriously.
- This time stand with your feet together.
- Place you hands out in front of you, bent at the elbow, together with fingers outstretched, as if these were the paws of a bunny.
- Bend your knees and jump in a small hop.
- Now keep jumping move your body in a circle as you jump.

My preference with my clients, especially when they are practising something they intend to say at a meeting, is to jump in 2 circles before immediately jumping into the body of the text they intend to say.

I have over 3000 business owners who I have worked with, all of whom do the bunny hop before they enter a business networking event. They do this so they can be fully present. They do this so they can be the best version of themselves when they are there. They do this so they can be of best service to the people in the room they are in.

This attitude of being of service to the room you are in is what makes it possible for my clients to make a bigger difference. Making a bigger difference and increasing the perception of value is what leads to greater income.

My challenge to you is this. Is it worth pretending to be a bunny for 30 seconds if the outcome is greater income?

Showing Your Passion

Show don't tell

Many of you may have seen an episode or 2 of The Apprentice. Whether you are in the UK and have watched Lord

Sugar, or Donald Trump in the US, you may recognise the experience I am going to discuss here.

Usually this occurs when the losing team are in the boardroom. That team has lost because they didn't put 100% of their passion into making the task a success.

In the UK, Lord Sugar often asks a candidate who has been brought back into the room and is now under consideration for firing, "Why should I keep you in this process?"

Immediately the answer comes back, "Don't fire me. I am SO passionate about this." They then go on to deliver a speech about their passion and how dedicated they are to making the best outcome happen for both themselves and Lord Sugar.

The question that this raises in me as a viewer is this. Where was this passion in all of the actions you took that brought you to this conversation now? Where was the passion when you were in the task, being recorded in action by a television crew, as you were self-sabotaging yourself and your team mates in a way that meant you failed the task?

To be direct, all of these speeches are pure bullshit.

In the world of film and theatre, the world of being paid to tell stories, you have the same idea.

I have spent far too many evenings in a theatre watching a play where the characters tell me what their emotional stories are, rather than show me. No-one is interested. There is nothing to learn about the state of being human in this way.

The same is true with The Apprentice people who tell people of their passion rather than show it in action. There is nothing more to learn about them. How can Lord Sugar trust them if they are unable to transmit that passion through action?

Perhaps you have had the experience of being told by someone that they love you and found it difficult to believe them. The reason, whether you realised or not, is that the action they demonstrated is not congruent with the words they spoke.

Remember what I said at the beginning of this book. It takes 23 seconds to form an opinion that is difficult to shift.

A switch flicks at 23 seconds in the listener's mind. The switch goes to either "Worth my Time" or "Not Worth My Time". This means that the words you say play very little part in the decision-making process.

There must be congruence. The 3 elements of this decision making are the words you say, the vocal tonality you use when you say them and all the nonverbal behaviour that backs up the other 2. If there is incongruence in any of the 3 layers then the unconscious mind of the listener can feel the "bullshit" that is coming from you.

Too many hours in business are spent with the mind and body disconnected. Too many meetings are run with disconnection. Too many meetings end up with the scheduling of another meeting, and no decisions made.

If you say you are the best at something, then let the whole of you back it up.

Once a client of mine took me to an event where several speakers (who she believed could do with my help) were speaking.

Unusually for me, this was an event where the speakers were all men. It was quite a macho selling space too, cajoling for Alpha positioning. Usually there is a lot of masculine energy backing this up (some of which is delivered in the 3rd Circle).

The host for the day stood up and gave a great, physically engaged, vocally engaged, rousing introduction to someone he declared passionately to be "the greatest mentor you could wish to get in the world of property".

Up onto the stage came a shambling man with his head bowed and a crooked neck. He stood, crunched up in the 1st circle and spoke with a very quiet voice. He spoke to his laptop more than he did to the audience.

"I am the best possible mentor you could get in the world of property" he repeated in this reedy, tiny voice.

The response was measurable in the room. We all knew this presentation was going to last 90 minutes. We all knew immediately it was not going to be engaging.

We all knew what we were in for.

A woman in the 2nd row, directly behind me, started gasping for breath, unaware why she was finding she could not breathe. She was falling in with the breath pattern of the man on the stage.*

The presentation was so bad that at the end, when he made an offer on the course he was selling and he told us all to go to the back of the room right now to sign up, not a single person moved.

If it was embarrassing before this, it was super embarrassing now.

Don't be like that man.

Be the person who makes their audience safe and engaged, because they were engaging themselves.

Make sure you stand when you speak. I make sure I am standing when I am attending any event. The reason is that you are more easily engaging when you speak. If a gesture you make comes as a result of a real feeling, then it will start from your core. If your gesture is not drawn from a real feeling, then it will start at the shoulder.

The problem with sitting down when you speak is that it is trickier for you to be connected to your core. This means many people who present an argument from a sitting position don't use their gesture to their best advantage. They can look as if they don't mean what they say.

To stand makes access to your centre easier and the words you speak more passionate, automatically.

If you want people to experience your passion, make sure you are standing. Forget about telling them all about your passion. Let your audience see it and feel it in your body and your voice.

---

* Humans are naturally rapport-building creatures. We do this without knowing at a conscious level. We build rapport with each other by falling into each other's breath patterns. When we are being led by someone in a group, the group will fall into the breath patterns of the person most dominant in that situation.

Becoming more productive

Life hacks for starting the day as a 10 out of 10

If I were in the room with you, I would ask you to raise your hand if you have ever had this experience.

Have you ever begun the day wondering what is the best way to begin? If so, has that thought allowed you to waste the time you have available to make a difference in the world?

1. Do your decision making in the evening before.
   The morning is a time for making stuff happen. Make your decisions about what "stuff" is going to happen the night before. Write it all down so it is clear and obvious in the morning when you come to work. Let there be no questions for the morning. This is what you are doing. It means beginning by going straight to the task. Make this your routine and you will become much more productive.

2. EAT that frog.
   Brian Tracy wrote a great book named "Eat That Frog". In his book, he proffered a question. What if we, every single one of us, had to eat a live frog to stay alive for the day? What if we had to do it every day? What time of day would we do it? If we waited until the end of the day, how much worse would that task get, waiting in our mind, reminding us of what is to come, thinking how vile an experience it will be? The best time to do this would be first thing in the morning. After all, there is very little worse that you could have to do during a day, so why not get it done so you can concentrate on tasks that would give you more satisfaction?
   When you write your list the night before, number the tasks in order of importance, and how closely the

task resembles the idea of eating a live frog. Choose the task that most feels like eating a live frog and underline it. Give it the biggest number on your list and make the commitment in writing that this task will be the first you tackle the next morning.

No matter how unpleasant the task, I guarantee you will feel accomplishment once it's done and you can move on to something easier.

3. Exercise before you begin work.

Commit to connecting your mind and body together before you enter your workspace. Get up, put on some workout clothes and get physical. Remember, at the beginning of this chapter how I said that running had become my "must" happen, rather than "nice to have" happen. The shorts, t-shirt and trainers are set by the bed. I have to feed the children and help get them ready to go to school. If you are reading this and thinking "I don't have time in the morning", then get up earlier. Find time for you. If you don't, you limit the possibilities of how much you can generate of value for those you love. I know I have to help feed and clothe my children and make a mug of coffee for my wife. I get up earlier to make sure that I can do all of this and get out there on the hill, regardless of the weather, and run.

Once done, my mind and body are connected. I am ready for work and can immediately hit the first task (decided the night before) with vigour.

4. Meditate. Clear Your Mind.

I have spent far too long in my life listening to the voice in my head set to sabotage my success. The hypothalamus is here to make sure you are alive, but it does not care how you feel. The hypothalamus knows that you can survive the condition you are in right now. It does not know yet that you can survive success, so it finds all sorts of ways to self-sabotage you. It does this by speaking to you in your head. (If you are sitting there thinking "What voice" then I say to you again, "That voice!")

If that voice keeps you awake at night, then cleanse yourself of it. Without proper sleep we are disadvantaged for the day.

Focus on creating a blank canvas for your day. Clear your mind. An image that comes strongly to me is one of my brain being cleansed of the dark thoughts that sit on it. Sometimes it is like a shower of water. It is an image I can go back to in order to cleanse my mind of thoughts and worries of the day.*

Mindfulness and meditation can be a useful method of cleansing. Perhaps there are meditations you can find on applications like Audible. Put them on your phone before bed and allow them to cleanse you.

Never underestimate the value of a good night's sleep.

Finding Your Peak State

*Around you are many things that are
shortcuts to being in a peak state*

You have a choice. You can choose to either be bigger than your circumstances, or not.

Harsh, I know. Also true.

---

* I am certainly not suggesting that my images will work for you. If they do, then great. It's your mind, not mine. Find imagery that will work for you to prevent you thinking the thoughts that sabotage and keep us from our sleep.

Every one of us faces a morning when we wake up and don't feel in the mood. Every one of us faces a meeting that we don't feel like attending, but have to anyway.

I have been there myself. Too long in my life I gave into my immediate feelings and chose not to be bigger than my circumstances. If I had been taught how to be mentally resilient when I was at drama school then maybe I would be telling you a different story now.

The other side of that coin is that I am super happy with the person I am now and every experience that got me to this point informs how I am now able to help so many people: clients, family, friends, business partners and others I bump into daily.

I understand the work that must be put in to rise above circumstances.

At first it can feel hard.

Until you realise that all around you are elements of life that you can harness to change your energy in an instant.

1. Fresh Air. Getting fresh air first thing in the morning, even if only for 5 minutes, gives your whole body access to fresh oxygen, a fully oxygenated frontal lobe, and it reminds you of how big this world is.

2. Exercise. Get exercise before you do anything else in your day. After 7 or 8 hours of lying down in a state of unconsciousness your body transforms into a state of wakefulness. Is it any surprise that navigating that metamorphosis can be tricky? Give your body the gift of exercise. Move that blood and get feeling into your extremities. Earlier in this chapter I talked about how taking 20 to 30 minutes a day to run has made a huge difference to the way I connect with the day and its tasks, and also long term it has been transformational to my wellbeing.

3. Music. What is your favourite piece of music? We are all connected to music. Regardless of whether we express emotion easily or not, we are connected at a deep emotional level to music. All music, whether we like it or not, creates emotion. Tune into the music that puts you in a tip top 10 out of 10 emotional state. Make sure you have it in your favourites or easy to access on your phone. As I write this book I have pieces of music in my headphones playing. The choices I make are dynamic and fast moving. Using this music I can write a chapter quickly and without distraction. Who would have thought that when I meet people who may or may not become clients, the success of that conversation seems to depend on whether I have listened to Pitbull's "Fireball" in the 4 minutes prior to the conversation? It's anecdotal, I know. However, I have measured the outcomes from when I do, and when I don't, and I get more "Yes" conversations when I do. It means the energy I show up with is 10 out of 10 regardless of whatever else may be going on in my life.

4. Food. You have heard of the expression, "Garbage in, Garbage Out". Nurture your body with your choices. Typically, in the western world, we eat far too much. The human body is not designed for 3 full meals a day, and the obesity we see globally is a reflection of that. Fasting may or may not be for you. It has worked extremely well for me alongside the running I mentioned earlier. Choose foods and drinks that release energy gently through the day and keep you alive to what is going on around you. Avoid food and drink that spike your energy and mean you drop energy as fast as you spike. I'm not an expert in this area, though I have many connections who are.

5.   Things to avoid energetically – Television. Television is one of the greatest sappers of energy globally. When I was a young actor sitting by the phone waiting for it to ring, I spent far too long sitting in front of a television watching things I had no interest in, waiting for something to happen. Nothing happens when you wait. You have to go out there and make something happen. I worked with one of the leading wealth management firms who said their biggest challenge for new franchisees was seeing them come out of a micromanaged position in a corporate firm and into a life where they were their own bosses only to find they didn't have the self discipline to switch off "Loose Women" on the television and start speaking to customers.

6.   Things to avoid – Social Media. Remove the apps from your phone. No ifs, no buts. Remove them. They are a rabbit hole. They are a rabbit hole dependent on creating feelings of depression and sadness so you remain in that rabbit hole. Remove them from your phone. Make a promise to yourself not to check in more than 3 times a day, and then at times that you don't have to be energised for the sake of others.

This is a little list of things around us, some of which are super helpful if we tap into them, some of which we definitely want to avoid.

The point of all of this is that you are in charge of you. You are in charge of your experience of life. No one else is. In this chapter are ideas and tips that anyone can choose to tap into in order to change their experience of life. Good luck to you all.

Chapter 6: Cats and Dogs
(the Metaphor For Success)

The Theory of Cats and Dogs

*The secret of influencing different
and difficult people*

I love Cats and Dogs theory. It is one of my favourite things to teach my clients.

One of the things I love about it is that the concept is so simple. There are only 2 options.

One of the other things I love about it is that is not difficult to make decisions about the appropriate action.

About 12 years ago I was working with the 12 regional directors of one of the UK's largest insurance firms. I, and a colleague, were delivering a 4-day seminar around showing up in sales. We were delivering days 1 and 2 in one month, giving the sales directors 1 month to put into action what they had learned, and then delivering days 3 and 4 the following month.

My colleague and I had been tasked with showing them how to deliver difficult, and sometimes unpalatable messages to their partners and clients.

At the end of day 2, as I was packing up, one of the regional directors, Alan, tapped me on the shoulder and asked if he might speak to me.

He told me of a meeting he had in his diary for the next day. It was with a broker he had been attempting to do some work with for at least 7 years. Alan told me that he had tried everything but this broker had never done any business with him. When Alan said everything he meant "special deals" and "discounts". Despite offering what Alan had thought were super attractive deals, this person had not been tempted into doing any business.

I sat him down and we had a discussion. Stop offering deals. Do this instead, I said. Then I explained to him the Cat and Dog theory and showed him how to apply it.

A month later we all met again and as part of our debrief we discussed what actions everyone had taken in the intervening month.

Alan raised his hand and told me that he had gone to the meeting the day after our conversation, done exactly as I had shown, and walked out of that meeting with a cheque for £44,000, money he had been chasing for 7 years.

If the thought of walking out of a meeting with £44k's worth of business is appealing to you, then read on.

Cats and Dogs was created by Michael Grinder, brother of John Grinder, the co-creator of Neuro-Linguistic Programming. After reading this you may want to dig further into Michael Grinder's work. There are several You Tube videos of Michael in action that I would advise anyone curious to proceed with this technique to check out.

Michael was tasked with finding the perfect teacher. By that I mean, what are the behaviours of the perfect teacher. The idea was to isolate behaviours that could be taught so that new teachers and teachers in training could be taught best practice.

Michael sat at the back of classrooms across both the UK and the US. He watched hundreds of teachers in action across primary and secondary schools.

Soon he lost interest in studying the behaviour of the teachers and began to concentrate on the behaviour of the students.

He found there were some classrooms where absolute silence reigned. The students were terrified of the teacher and no learning took place.

He found there were classrooms where absolute chaos reigned. The teachers were popular but the students were out of control. Again, no learning took place.

He also found there were classrooms where there was just enough silence to allow a teacher to impart information and just enough openness to allow the students to enquire and engage with the work.

What were these teachers doing that the others were not? Now we returned his attention to the teachers and studied their behaviours.

From these studies he came up with the metaphor of Cats and Dogs.

The idea is that all of us have aspects of Cat and Dog inside us and depending on the context of who we are with and what is happening in a room, we will choose to be more Cat or more Dog.

The advantage of this is that we are studying behaviour rather than personality. I'm sure many of you will have completed a personality assessment at some point in their professional life and had the experience of having that assessment read back to you, agreeing with some of it and wildly disagreeing with other aspects of it.

You also know, if you have attempted to study people's personality in that first 23-second window we know so well in this book, that it can be difficult. Often, to define what someone is like takes time.

Behaviour rather than personality is immediate feedback. People reveal their needs through behaviour rather than personality.

If we are examining behaviours instead then our decisions can be immediate. We can choose to give people what they need, if we want.

If we were in an interview for an important job with a big

pay rise attached, do you think it would be helpful to see what the body language of your interviewers is telling you about what is really going on in the room?

If you had an employee in your team who you needed to have a direct discussion with, do you think it helpful if you can hear, via the tonal choices in their voice, what is really happening for them?

The ideas that Cats and Dogs represent is Credibility and Approachableness.

Sometimes we are in social situations with others where we need to accentuate our professional credibility and in others we accentuate our rapport building and welcoming skills.

Sometimes we can be in social situations when we are nervous. There might be some stakes around the outcomes of the meeting. Those stakes might be financial. They might be reputational. They might be both. In these situations we are likely to fall back on stress defaults, especially if we are fearful around the idea of not being liked.

If you are afraid of not being liked, or concerned about what other people think, then perhaps leadership is not for you. Alternatively, you might be willing to make some changes and work on yourself so it is not the case that you care.

Dogs are social animals. Dogs hang out in packs. Dogs care wildly about whether they are liked by their owners.

Think back to when you owned a dog, or someone you know owned a dog.

What happens when you say "Walkies!!!" to a dog? The dog gets excited, doesn't it. The dog jumps around and wags their tail. After you have had that reaction, you don't then ask the dog "Where do you fancy going? The shops? The park?" That would confuse the dog. The dog actively wants you to make the decision for them.

Perhaps you have owned a cat in your life. Or known someone who has.

What happens if you say "Walkies!!!" to a cat? What kind of reaction are you likely to have? The cat is likely to walk away in disgust at the thought of you making decisions for them. After all, Cat owners, you all have cat flaps in your back door. No dog owner has a dog flap.

Dogs are more loyal. Cats are more independent.

If we use this metric, where do you think Cats and Dogs sit in the average organisation?

The social science tells us that the average split in a corporate organisation is 70% Dog and 30% Cat.

Most Dogs are happy to sit at the bottom of an organisation doing a great job delivering a task, and delivering it well, all for the reward of treats and congratulations from their bosses. Most Dogs are happy to be working in teams.

Most Cats will move quickly upwards in companies because they are independent and work best in solitary roles. They are also hierarchical and love to know where they sit within the company hierarchy.

Most Cats will also find there is a glass ceiling for them where they stop and remain stuck. This is usually because they have operational skills but lack the people skills necessary for senior management.

In order for a Cat to traverse that ceiling they are going to have to develop some Dog skills.

We call the behavioural flexibility needed for senior management, Dat or Cog. You have to have aspects of both to be there, otherwise you will never communicate ideas in a way that the Dogs at the bottom of the organisation will understand or be able to commit to doing.

We can see clearly that, if you are ambitious, being in Dog mode the majority of the day is not going to help you. As a dog you can do an excellent job of work delivery. However, being in Dog mode will teach the management that you are not a serious player. You will be referred to as "lightweight" as many of my clients have experienced when they first come to me.

We can see that Cat mode will work well if you are moving up from the bottom of a company to a management role. We can also see that if you are primarily in Cat mode that you will lack the skills to recognise what others underneath you need in order to function best. If you can't do that, you will never elevate your team members in order that you, yourself, can be elevated to your next role.

We can also see that behavioural flexibility is the key to moving to the top.

All of this is equally true if you run your own business.

If you run your own business you may find, as salespeople often do, that you are in Dog mode a lot in order to build rapport with clients and colleagues. You may also find that being in Dog mode smothers you and prevents growth. In order to grow you need your Cat. In order to bring in staff so you can grow your business, you need to be in Cat mode some of the time.

You will also find that if you have staff and you want to elevate them so you can move your business to the next level, you are going to need behavioural flexibility too.

So how do we recognise a Cat or a Dog through their behaviour?

What's Your Experience of Others?

Shift the stories you tell yourself about other people, and your own abilities to connect

The stories we tell ourselves about the people we meet and our relationship with them is coloured by our own experiences of life. People are often like other people. We waste a great deal of time trying to work out what people are like.

Maybe you have been on the receiving end of a communication from someone that has surprised you. The way they behaved, or articulated something might be a shock. You may think you have a friendly relationship with a boss until something goes wrong. Then they approach you with a different voice and their face suddenly looks stern. Immediately this friend becomes someone unfamiliar.

When something like this happens, often we can let it shock us to the core. If we are high on the agreeableness scale, then we will feel this deeply, often characterising it as betrayal.

If we look at these so-called betrayals through the lens of Cat and Dog it may help us to have a greater understanding of the other person's behaviour.

In a work environment, a manager may have to adopt a more direct Cat persona to represent their role and act in the interests of the company. When in Cat mode nothing is personal. Work is a game. If you are on the receiving end of some Cat feedback whilst you are in Dog mode, then you will take it personally. The fact that the manager has represented themselves as a fellow Dog to you in the past works against their credibility when they must become Cat with you.

You may have to develop your own Cat to protect yourself from Cats who are above you in the hierarchy. Cats breathe deeply in the stomach, lessening the physical impact of any emotions coursing through the blood.

I ended the previous section posing a question about how we recognise a Cat or a Dog.

Here is the answer.

Once you know how to spot one, start looking at people in your life.

Please also bear in mind that when you are looking at this, you are looking at behaviour rather than personality. This is purely about what they are doing right now! At home, or in a social environment they may behave completely differently. Context is everything.

A Dog just wants to be liked.

When a Dog comes into work, they will take ages to get down to doing a work task. They will hang out checking in on everyone before settling down to work.

They build rapport constantly. They will empathise with any experience you may mention. They value friendship above all.

Their desk, if they have a desk, will be littered with photographs. They will bring their personal lives into work. You will know all about their tastes in food, television, sport and friends. Their lives will be an open book.

A Dog will do almost anything to avoid conflict.

They will be informal in how they dress and how they stand.

Dogs work best in teams and are not keen on having to make decisions.

A Cat, on the other hand, does not care about friendship. They value respect.

A Cat values clarity and logic.

They focus on feedback. Unlike Dogs, rapport is not a consideration. Being direct and telling people how it is matters.

Because of that they are always clear about expectations.

They create formal outcomes and stick to them like glue.

They have a more formal style in dress and how they represent themselves physically.

When you read these descriptions, are you thinking of people you know or people you work with?

Let's dig deeper and make things easier for you.

I'm going to show you how to recognise a Cat or a Dog just by looking at them.

The approachable Dog leans forward. They stand with their weight to one side, leaning more on one leg than the other. Sitting, they may proffer one cheek over the other as they lean to the side.

Whilst listening to you their head will bob up and down. They will nod and make listening sounds. A listening sound might be something like "hmmm, oh yes, hmmm, hmmm, oh, that happened to me too". This is all about the building of rapport. Watching 2 Dogs together build rapport by nodding in synch offering listening sounds in a constant score of "hmmm"-ing can be funny to see.

When they speak, they take forever to get to the point. They go "all around the houses" as we used to say in Scotland describing a bus route that takes a long time to get between 2 close-by termini. They Segway into a new thought mid sentence.

When they speak they will primarily be using the heart voice.

When they gesture they will be using the heart voice, the voice of rapport building.

It will almost always sound as if they are seeking information.

Who is coming to mind as you hear this description?

Alternatively a Cat will stand absolutely straight, with their hand sitting balanced on top of their spine.

When they listen, their head will be completely still and they will make no noise. For a Cat this is true listening. The way a Dog listens to another is pure white noise to a Cat.

When they speak they will use the smallest number of words to get directly to the point. Often a Cat will omit any personal pronouns.

When they speak they will primarily be using the Warrior Voice.

When they gesture they will be gesturing palm down. Palm down can be anything from the hands parallel to each other with fingers pointing toward each other up to a full palm downward gesture.

It will almost always sound as if they are delivering instruction.

Now that you know this, I have a question and a task for you.

Firstly, start observing. Become a mini-Sherlock Holmes. Start looking and listening to people, especially the people who you don't feel you have the best relationship with at work.

Write down how you think this knowledge could be valuable to help you build rapport with those you have trouble with. Identify what you can start doing to change these relationships.

What Do Cats Need?

Remember that curiosity killed the cat

Cats need credibility, and they need it fast. This is the advantage of understanding the first 23 seconds. We often make the mistake of thinking that credibility is about the words that we say, rather than the way that we say it. Time is the valuable commodity and Cats understand this clearly.

Companies have come to me and said, "We'd like you to work with one of our managers. We love her, but she is too lightweight." This perception of "lightweight" comes not from the performance in the role. It comes from the perception surrounding ways of behaving.

Cats reveal themselves through their body language and their voice. Facial movement will be small if at all. They will primarily be in the Warrior Voice, to the point in their speech and most gestures will be played with the palm down.

If you are someone who wants to impress up the management chain and has a Cat boss, then pay attention.

Cats and Dogs miss each other because their behaviours read as white noise to the other. All the nodding that Dogs do with each other drives Cats insane. What a show, what a waste of time, goes the voice in their head.

Cats need to feel safe in the company of others, like anyone. The behaviours they choose to exhibit, and the behaviours they seek to see in others are all based around the idea of being surrounded by people who make them feel safe.

I once had a client, a female department head, who worked for one of the biggest building societies in the country. I was sitting at home one day when my phone went, and it was my client. "Help!" she exclaimed. "I need you to come up to Scotland tomorrow morning first thing. I have just destroyed my career!"

I booked my plane up to Scotland, taxi into the centre of Edinburgh and waited for my client at the dance studio I normally used.

She arrived in a panic. This was her story.

Yesterday morning she arrived at work and went to the in-house coffee shop. There was a queue and she took her place in the queue. A moment later she noticed that the man in front of her was the company CEO. "Aha!" she thought to herself. "This is my opportunity to gain some visibility." She then tapped the CEO on the shoulder, he turned, and off she went into full-on Dog mode.

The CEO was in Cat mode. He stands there silently and still. As my client went full Dog, moving around, using the full range of her voice, big smiles, gesturing wildly, he gave her back nothing.

She stopped. Looking in his eyes, she thought to herself "He's not getting me!"

Her response to this thought is to go even bigger with her Dog. Louder, brasher, gesturing even more wildly.

Eventually he starts to step back, nearly bumping into the person in front of him in the queue. Then he makes his excuses and leaves the queue, without a coffee, to go back to his office.

My client got her coffee and got to walk back to her own office wondering what the heck just happened. Because she is in Dog mode she takes everything very personally. So she sits in her office chair catastrophising how badly this will affect her career.

Her career was absolutely fine, it turned out. I did a session on her breathing and brought her back into 2nd circle. Once in 2nd circle she could see things as they were, rather than worse.

Cats don't take things personally. Business is a game for them. Something happens or something is said. It is gone within seconds. That Cat's mind has left it behind. For a Dog, that experience will sit, rent free in their mind for a long time.

At the time I wasn't aware of the Cat/Dog metaphor. When

I first learned it, I understood how this happened for my client.

Dogs build rapport with each other by doing what we call in the coaching world "matching". Matching means that if one nods then so does the other. They match body language in order to show the other they are in rapport with them and their experiences.

Cats build rapport by testing and mismatching. Dogs get confused and worried when they are in the presence of a mismatching Cat. This always happens when I teach this to a group of people in a workshop. The Cats in the room will always attempt to prove the rules are wrong. They will do this by demonstrating their mismatching. If one person crosses their legs, the Cat will uncross.

Cats are amenable to the idea of Dogs sitting below them in a management chain. Certainly they will not entertain the idea of a Dog at the same level as them.

How do you entertain a dog?

You go to a park with your dog and you throw a ball. The dog retrieves the ball and gives it back to you with the expectation that you are going to throw it again. That dog will be happy for you to do that for the next hour without deviation.

You can't do that with a cat? Cats are independent, remember?

How would you play with a cat?

You might dangle something on the end of a piece of string, in order to activate curiosity in a cat. The cat becomes curious and steps up to paw at the item you are dangling.

What would happen if you then gave the item to the cat?

It would get bored and leave it be.

However, what happens if you pull the item away from the cat, just centimetres away from the cats having contact? Curiosity is increased.

There is a famous phrase. "Curiosity killed the Cat." This is true. With curiosity the Cat becomes a Dog.

Cats like to be decision makers. They don't like others

making decisions for them. That's good because Dogs really don't like making decisions.

Imagine you have a Cat boss who has given you a task like, what are the best pens to use in the office? How might you create curiosity out of this task?

Perhaps you go back to the boss with 3 different pen options. Perhaps you have a preference yourself about the one you want to use. Instead of proffering this as the best option, you might want to tease your boss by suggesting "I'm pretty sure you are not going to want this one." Immediately a Cat will want to see that one, the one you are trying to count out, because they don't want you to be making decisions for them.

Take that idea and write down how you might create curiosity using a task that you might be given by a Cat boss.

Don't Lead Dogs as a Dog

*There is nothing worse, as a dog,
than being led by another dog*

If you want to be a leader then you don't want to do it as a Dog. There may be opportunities when your Dog persona works for you. They will be few and far between.

Dogs do not like being lead by Dogs. It makes them nervous. A team of Dogs may moan about their Cat boss. The Cat boss will make them feel a lot safer than a Dog boss.

I once worked as a new business developer for a group of young creatives being led by a CEO who was totally Dog.

He was a fabulous man to be with when things were going well. A total nightmare when things were not.

He laid bare the fullness of his life, his stresses and his pains. He articulated them, putting them on the table at meetings in front of every member of staff.

The young creatives were mainly in Dog mode. This level of openness from up top terrified them. So they shut down. They worked to rule. They were not excited about new projects. This created a barrier in the studio that eventually led to the CEO retiring from the company and the company being sold off to a bigger company. None of the staff survived the sale.

Most people who are really comfortable in Dog mode are resistant to the idea of building up their Cat. They believe that they will make better leaders by remaining in Dog and appealing to the friendship within the team. That works well when things go well. When things go badly it will all go awry. Teams of Dogs need to come together under the banner of certainty offered by a Cat leader. If your leader is a Dog, then at the first sign of trouble, it is every Dog for themselves.

Don't fall into the trap of thinking that nothing needs to change if you are promoted.

It's not unusual to look at someone who has been recently promoted and think to yourself "Well, they have changed!" It is correct. They have changed. Quite rightly too. There are behaviours that are appropriate at every management stage within a company. There are also behaviours that are not.

Here is an exercise for you to do. This will identify for you what needs to change to move you forward from where you are, and get you paid according to the appropriate value you could be bringing.

- What's the next stage of your career journey? Have you identified yet where you want to be next?
- What needs to change from you in order that that may happen?
- Are you more Cat or more Dog?
- Imagine you have already been promoted. Imagine what it will be like to be in your new job. How will it change your relationship with your colleagues?
- Write down the behaviours you are exhibiting now

that you believe would be inappropriate to demon-strate in this new job. Make the list as large as you can.
- Choose the 3 that appear to be most important to you.

Make a promise to yourself now. Start working on these now. Are you too Dog in your communication? If yes, start building up your Cat.

Are you too Cat in your communication? Start building your Dog options too. How could you build better rapport so you have buy-in from colleagues when you get promoted?

Becoming DAT or COG

Behavioural flexibility is the key to
moving into the elite circles

There comes a time when even the most ardent credible Cat gets stuck.

Usually, Cats rise quickly in an organisation. Focused solely on the task, they engineer their career in a targeted fashion. Dogs look on and call them ruthless. Dogs rarely move far forward in a company because they don't focus themselves behind a vision of a future. Dogs find comfort in the idea that every day is the same. It gives the illusion of immortality. It stops many of them thinking about their own mortality and how little time we have on this planet to carve out something for ourselves.

So the bottom-line message of this chapter for the Dogs reading this is, Be More Cat. Find a way to add a Cat persona to aspects of your day.

Cats get stuck just underneath their own glass ceiling. This is the glass ceiling of influence. This glass ceiling sits just underneath the boardroom.

Because Cats are usually great at making things happen, they are usually not so hot on interpersonal communication. They end up with a bad rap from the bottom of the management chain who accuse them of not listening.

In order for Cats to move past the glass ceiling they have to discover how to be more Dog. Ironic, you might think, since the Dogs sit at the bottom of the management chain. The thing that is needed now is leadership. Leadership is the ability to influence those below you in the management chain so that they take the action you desire them to take, so your company grows in the way it wants to. Leadership is highly prized in any ambitious company and the senior leadership are always looking for the people to elevate up to their level. At a senior leadership level, redundancy is always on their minds. Who can we get to do this task, so I no longer have to?

My instruction for Cats is, develop your Dog. Learn how to be more Dog on a daily basis. Everything in this book revolves around the idea that it takes 4 to 6 weeks of little but often practice to form a new behavioural habit.

To operate at the top table you have to be behaviourally flexible. You have to have the flexibility to be Cat when it is right to be Cat, and Dog when it is right to be Dog.

The most successful people round a boardroom table are DATs or COGs. They have aspects of both and they understand that charisma is being able to move from one to the other on the basis of who you are with and what it is they need right now.

That is the metaphor that is Cats and Dogs. Enjoying playing with this? At least one of my clients has an extra £300k coming into her income stream that she absolutely would not have without developing her Cat. If the thought of that outcome works for you, get practising.

Don't forget that Michael Grinder, the creator of this, has posted a number of short videos on YouTube and his own website, www.michaelgrinder.com, where he demonstrates how to build your credibility with the big Cats at the top table.

Chapter 7: Mindset

The Voices in Your Head

You can't concentrate on something
without concentrating on it

Now that we have spent the last 6 chapters focusing on the physical experience and your perceptions around the physical experience of others, we move our focus to what is happening internally.

Ultimately our understanding of the world and our experience of all things in this world depends on what we tell ourselves inside our own head.

We can't control what happens to us in life. We can control how we choose to respond to that which his happening.

It is also true that whenever emotion is high, intelligence is low. The more the emotional state you are in, the less the likelihood you can find a way out of the experience you are having.

Tony Robbins has a saying which is "You can't concentrate on something without concentrating on it." Your brain will give you what it believes you want on the basis of what you are thinking about.

I will give you an example.

I once worked with the CEO of a pharmaceutical company. The company was super-successful with a staff of around 50 people. The CEO, Mark, had worked his way up through what he called "the shop floor" to running the company. He was very much a man of principle and one of the most important principles he had was one of consistent honesty.

He believed that transparency in business dealings was essential. Transparency that worked its way down to the shop floor.

Do you know the story of when President John F Kennedy, who I mention earlier in this book, visited Cape Canaveral whilst the Apollo missions were being prepped so the USA could win the space race?

During his visit he saw a cleaner with a mop cleaning the floor of the reception area. Because JFK wanted everyone to feel included, he walked to the man and asked, "What is it you do around here?"

The cleaner turned to him and replied, "Like everyone else here, Mr President, I am helping to put a man on the moon."

So my client, Mark, had similar feelings around making sure every member of staff felt included in the big picture.

Every Monday morning would begin, 9am, with Mark addressing every member of staff with everything that was going on with the company.

That is until one Monday he stood up on stage, opened his mouth to speak, and his mind went blank.

He stood onstage, silent, with his mouth gaping wide open, whilst 50 people looked at him, waiting!

20 seconds felt like an eternity to Mark, who turned to Steve, his No 2, sitting in the front row of the audience. "You take over, Steve" he said and then promptly ran away from the stage to his office.

Poor Steve, unprepared, stepped up onto the stage and made something up on the spot.

Mark went back to his office and said to himself, "This must never happen again."

So he prepared like crazy for the next Monday, focused on the content being perfect.

Next Monday he stood on stage and froze a second time. This time Steve was prepared with something to deliver.

This went on for several weeks because I was called in to

resolve the situation. In resolving it, which I did, we used all the exercises that I have shown you in the book. One thing really stood out that is relevant for what we are discussing in this chapter.

In our first meeting I asked many questions, one of which was this: "How do you begin preparing for the presentation?"

"Oh that's easy" he said. "As soon as I come offstage and start thinking about the next presentation I go straight to my whiteboard and I write this."

He grabbed a pen, scrubbed out whatever was on his whiteboard and wrote this.

"THIS MUST NOT BE SHIT".

Forgive the language.

Notice how you feel when you read this. How does it make you think?

Are you aware that the brain cannot accommodate a negative? If you want to delete something from your mind you have to create it in the first place.

If you want to know what I mean then obey this instruction. Whatever you do now, DO NOT, I repeat, DO NOT, think of a blue elephant in a tree.

See! How many of you saw that blue elephant in your minds eye? I imagine, most of you.

This means that if you concentrate on what you do not want to happen, your brain has no way of knowing that it is what you don't want to happen.

Most people prior to an interview are likely to imagine, in their minds eye during the 15 minutes prior to going into the interview room, all the possible ways they could screw up in the interview. Lovingly, we will imagine this in the finest detail. Our brain does this to us as a defence mechanism. It is to shield us from disappointment. Unfortunately, after a full 15 minutes of imagining, with the exultation to self of "Don't screw up" as we walk into the interview, we self-fulfil that prophecy. Our brain now thinks that the screw up is what we want, after all, if we didn't why would be spend 15 minutes thinking about it. The brain usually delivers to us what we are thinking of.

You can't concentrate on something without concentrating on it.

As it was for Mark, my client. He was spending 5 full weekdays staring at this white board.

"THIS MUST NOT BE SHIT".

His brain can only read the worst "THIS MUST BE SHIT".

After 5 full days of looking at this, how do you imagine that Mark would be feeling? Pretty shit, right!

When he steps out onto the stage on Monday morning he is so steeped in the concentration of "SHIT" that his brain can't help but deliver what it believes Mark is looking for.

Whatever you concentrate on you will receive.

Maybe it is time to start concentrating on how things will go right.

What do you think?

Make a list for yourself of every opportunity you can think of where your brain may have self-sabotaged you by virtue of what you concentrated on.

Conquering Your Fears

The key to conquering your fears is
what you tell yourself each day
"Most of the worst days in my life never
actually happened" – Mark Twain

I've loved that quote from Mark Twain for several years. I come back to it on a weekly, if occasionally daily, basis.

You cannot control your circumstances. The only thing you can control is your response to those circumstances.

It has been a harsh lesson to learn, and I have to keep

learning it. I say this because when emotions are high intelligence is low. To think I went through this world for almost 50 years without an understanding of this.

I've known this fact and worked on myself to a very deep level because I let my heart rule my head far too often and made several bad decisions as a result.

Most of us make bad decisions when emotion is high. Emotion is often high because of the circumstances of life. Remember, either we believe life is happening TO us, or we believe it is happening FOR us. Those are diametrically opposed views of the world. If you believe the first you will see the events of your life rather differently. You will ask many questions in your head: "Why is this happening to me?" "How come this always happens to me?" "Will I ever be rewarded for all my work?"

As we discovered earlier it is a rabbit hole from which the only escape is to change mindset.

The other side of the coin is around the belief that life happens for us. If we believe this then the questions we ask of ourselves are rather different. "What am I meant to learn here?" is the main focus. "What do I need to do differently to obtain a different result?" might be another.

I'd like to share a simple life hack that I use for when I am faced with difficult conversations or feel some fear around taking action.

The hypothalamus will want to imagine the worst in order to stop us stepping out of our comfort zone and into the danger zone. Remember, that nothing can change whilst we are in the comfort zone.

Perhaps you can already think of a call or a meeting you need to have soon, the thought of which fills you with fear. Perhaps you are already trying to think of reasons not to make the call. There might be other things you can do to put off making the call.

When I am faced with these calls, and I still am – and I still get scared at the thought of a call which may end with someone being displeased with me or what I have to say – I run 3 visualisations for the sake of my unconscious mind. I do this so it has context around what is the worst that can happen.

This is an adaptation of an exercise from the world of NLP that is called a "Circle of Excellence".

In my mind's eye I throw a movie screen up on a wall that I can face. It is an imaginary movie screen. I can see it only via the imagination of my mind's eye.

I am going to run 3 movies in my mind's eye before I make the call.

In the first movie I will imagine the meeting going the worst possible way. I really dig deep and extrapolate what is the worst outcome of the call possible. At the end I make sure I see myself putting down the phone, coming away from the call and moving on to the next thing I will do in life. It is important to see that my life will not be worse off because of that call. Nothing has changed. I will go to put the kettle on exactly as I would if the call went any other way. Or I pick up the phone to make my next call, exactly as I would have done anyway. It is important to show this to the unconscious mind. You will survive.

It is important to do this one first. The hypothalamus wants to go here. Let it. Get it out the way. Feel each moment, immerse yourself in the feeling, in the fear. Then let it all go.

After this I tear down the imaginary cinema screen with my hand, and then set up a new clean one.

The second movie I will run is the call going the best possible way. I imagine whatever is the best outcome possible for me and for the person I am talking to. I see myself celebrating creating that outcome. Again, feel the emotions you would feel if it were actually happening right now.

Then tear down that movie screen and set up a third.

In this third and final movie before we make the call, I will imagine myself and the other person in a bubble. I will imagine with as much detail as I can the bubble around us both.

The bubble has to have some density to it so you can see that nothing outside the bubble can get in and nothing inside the bubble can get out. Whatever happens with this call, it can only affect the rest of my life if I choose for it to.

This will help my unconscious mind to understand the distance between my emotions and the outcomes I want to happen in the call. That distance will ground your breathing, lower your heart rate and internal temperature. You will be ready.

Then I tear down the final movie screen and pick up the phone.

This is my life hack. This is the system I use to deal with any difficult conversation.

I wish you lots of luck, of your own creation, using this to master your fear.

Training Your Voice

*The 3rd Eye is open to being trained
as an asset rather than a critic*

For most people, the 3rd eye, that voice in your head (the one that just said, "What voice?"), is the difference between being successful or not.

Whilst you are breathing in the chest the 3rd eye is in the full employ of the hypothalamus. It will show you exactly what you need to see to be dissuaded from taking action.

When I was young there was a fashion among film directors of thrillers to use a "fisheye" lens. This lens was designed to make the image look skew-whiff (an 18th century Scots expression). The fish-eye lens makes things in the centre of the image unnaturally large and things at the edge of the image look smaller. It also rounded the image so that things with a straight line would look curved. It would curve parts of people's faces in the centre of the lens, so that they would have huge foreheads. It was usually used to indicate some sort of "unhinged" experience of a character. Often we would see this lens being used if we were seeing things either in a dream or from the 1st person perspective of the "killer" in the film.

I mention the fisheye lens because when you are breathing in the chest, the 3rd eye does something similar to all of us. When we are in a physical state of anxiety we see the world through a fish-eye lens. Problems are bigger than they really are. We start to expect trouble and problems, and low and behold, the world gives us exactly that.

Tony Robbins says you should see the world as it is, not worse, not better.

In the 1st circle we are likely to see the world worse than it is. In the 3rd circle, we are likely to be blind to problems that are coming toward us, due to the show we are putting on.

It is only in the 2nd circle that we can see the world as it truly is, give the right amount of import to the problems in front of us, because we see them in their real dimensions.

The baseline state of your 3rd eye is as an unremitting critic. An unremitting critic will tell you bad things about yourself regardless of the state you are in. Remember, the hypothalamus does not care how you feel. It only intends to stop you doing things it has identified as dangerous.

Get your 3rd eye used to being in the 2nd circle with you. Use your own internal voice to tell it to stop giving you unremitting criticism. When you hear that voice in your head, stop it in its tracks with the other voice. Gain some balance. Soon the 3rd eye will begin a journey of recalibration. It can and is open to being retrained as an asset in your life, telling you when real danger looms and showing it to you without the added lens of distortion.

When you hear that voice in your head, lie down. Lie on the floor, preferably with your head slightly elevated by putting a book under it. Raise your knees so your legs are bent and the soles of your feet are flat on the floor. With your spine now as flat and straight as it can be, give your attention to your breathing. Focus on lowering the breath deep into the stomach. Slow down your breathing by giving your attention to the muscles in the v of the groin. Feel the muscles opening as you breathe in, closing as you breathe out.

This will ground the breath, wake up your abdominal muscles and help flood your frontal lobe with the oxygen you need to think clearly.

Try this exercise now or at your earliest opportunity. Spend 10 minutes in the position described and note down how differently you think in relation to the challenges in your life.

Do this regularly so your body can work out that this is the way we do things now.

What's Stopping You?

Is it money, is it time, is it you
are too tired, is it bullshit?

If you like getting your motivation vibe going, then there is a YouTuber I heartily recommend. His name is Ben Lionel Scott. He has a video entitled "What's Stopping You?". Just stick that in the YouTube search engine and it should find it for you.

Motivation never lasts. Which is why, like bathing, I recommend it daily.

Life has a habit of throwing things in the way of our plans. We have a choice how we respond to this. We can either choose to be bigger or smaller than our problems.

Everything has perspective.

I heard my 12-year-old son say to himself the other day, "Why does this always happen to me? I am so unlucky!"

He said this in relation to his character in a video game coming to an untimely end, regularly in a period of 10 minutes.

When he said this to himself he absolutely meant it. That was his perspective at the time. He felt unlucky. He believed he was unlucky.

Yet he is remarkably privileged by virtue of having a roof over his head, a loving family, enough money in the bank to feed, clothe and indulge him in his chosen pastimes. These items alone put my son in the top 8% of the world, wealth wise.

The danger is that having articulated this sense of being unlucky, that carries forward from a virtual world to the real one.

Suffering is part of life. It need not become the central experience of life, unless you choose to let it.

Let me tell you a story of a client of mine, Sabrina. Sabrina is one of my clients from the UK's National Health Service. Sabrina and I worked for a year together because she was struggling to position herself as a leader in a director role. By the end of that year we spent together, she had achieved the director role she wanted. Great for her and great for me, because she is now my number 1 advocate and, as we speak, we are creating a programme for the senior leadership team which will be rolled out on an annual basis.

When I first met Sabrina there were a number of issues that plagued her. One of the reasons she believed she wasn't being considered for a role above where she was is that she has a serious, occasionally debilitating, physical condition.

Sabrina has Ehlers-Danlos Syndrome. Ehlers-Danlos Syndrome (or EDS as I shall now call it) is a rare condition that affects connective tissue in the body. Connective tissue that provides support to skin, blood vessels and bone.

Some of the symptoms include hypermobility, easily breaking skin, constant joint pain, dizziness and sharp increases in heart rate when standing.

Sabrina had a number of those symptoms and had arranged with her management that she should deliver a number of days of work each week from home because of the physical strain on her.

When we first started work, the story sat in her head that despite her passion for everything she did and despite her physical commitment to creating great outcomes for the Trust, that no one would consider her for a position more senior than she had. She also was telling herself a story in her head about not taking risks. This story related to needing the security of her income as it was, and not taking a risk that might threaten that.

In the first 3 months of our work together we did a lot around the Alexander Technique in order to change her experience of her own body. She found them to be a revelation. She could live differently. She didn't have to be in pain all the time. She didn't have to hold herself up by holding on to the side of a table or chair. Her mindset began to change.

Thank goodness too. I say that because of what happened when she applied for the director role later in the year.

It would have been easy for her to step back into the fear around the syndrome she lives with daily. The voice in her head telling her she wasn't good enough, she wouldn't be able to do the job.

Imagine being placed in a position where that was happening not only in your own head, but out of others' mouths as well.

As she was going through the interview process, she had a visit on 2 different occasions from senior male leaders in the Trust. In both cases they parked themselves on the side of her desk, adopting a caring demeanour and voice.

"You don't really want this job, do you? You don't SERI-OUSLY think you can do it, what with your illness, do you?"

She must have been doing something very right to have rattled the feathers of those particular men.

Can you honestly say that if you had visits from colleagues who said things like that to you, that would not have let that affect you? Can you honestly say that those voices would not echo in your head like a tape recording?

Thank goodness Sabrina's mindset had changed, because those were the words she was telling herself at the beginning of our process.

Sabrina was steadfast and was rewarded by a director role that makes her one of the biggest decision makers in the Trust. She has since embarked on a programme to change the culture of the Trust, and then market that out to change the culture of other Trusts that may have lost their way. The difference she is making now is at least 10 times the level she could have when we first met.

All because she chose not to listen to the voices in her head.

If ever you wake up in the morning and think to yourself, "I can't do this, I haven't had enough sleep." Or "I haven't got enough money to do any of the things I want in life", or the oft repeated, "I don't have enough time", then I would ask you to spend some time looking at the videos of Nick Vujicic, who has created a remarkable, fulfilling, and happy life despite not having any limbs. (Check out www.lifewithoutlimbs.org) A few moments with Nick usually helps us find a little perspective.

Nothing that life had thrown at Sabrina, Nick or millions of others stopped them. Nothing need stop them. Nothing needs to stop you.

Stories You Tell Yourself

Work out where and who your stories
come from and then give them back

This chapter has really been about the way that stories can adversely affect us. Stories we tell ourselves that stop us taking action.

We know that the more successful people in life have more energy than the majority on this planet. We also know that with more energy you are going to DO more. That means taking action and taking more action than most.

Every one of us has the same 24 hours a day, the same 1440 minutes a day, the same 86400 seconds per day. Richard Branson has the same number of seconds in a day that you do. Are you making the same difference in the world that he is? I appreciate that some of you may not like what Richard Branson is doing in the world. Can we at least admit to ourselves that he accomplishes a deal of stuff with his day?

If not, would you like to accomplish more with your day?

To make a bigger difference we must get the limiting belief stories out of our head and send them back to where they belong. Because the stories are usually not yours.

Usually, the stories we tell ourselves about what we can and cannot do are hand-me-downs from your family. Maybe they belong to your mum or dad. Certainly, stories we tell ourselves about money do.

Think of a story that you tell yourself that stops you from moving forward. Perhaps it is a story that keeps you in bed rather than get up and face the day. Perhaps it is a story that stops you picking up the phone or arranging a meeting. You choose. Choose something that, assuming you get past the story, will move you forward in some way.

Close your eyes.

Ask your unconscious mind to travel back in time to the moment in your life when this story first was embedded.

Don't try and make something happen here. We don't want to involve the conscious mind at all. The conscious mind won't have a clue when this story was embedded. The more you try and involve the conscious mind the less chance you have of finding and resolving this. Trust that your unconscious mind is working just fine by itself.

When the unconscious mind has found the answer it will find a way to let you know. Perhaps you will feel it in a physical experience; a warmth or a lowering of temperature.

Perhaps you will get this in a thought. Wait until you have received a message from your unconscious mind.

Keep your eyes closed after you have received this message. If you could visualise this moment your unconscious mind has discovered, what would it be?

When I did this recently I could immediately see myself aged 4 in the room I shared with my 1-year-old sister in Portobello, Edinburgh.

Do I often remember that room and that time? No. Was this an accurate representation of that room in that house back in 1967? Heck, I have no idea. It's an image or memory that my unconscious mind has delivered to me in that moment. As such, I trust that this image is being brought to me for a reason.

Keep visualising as if you were a camera on a drone in a movie. Examine the scene from every possible angle. See what your younger self is seeing. See it from the perspective of whatever your younger self is looking at. Step into your younger self and allow yourself to feel whatever they are feeling right now in this moment.

Find out from your exploration, like a detective, what was that moment the story was embedded.

Once you know you must speak to the younger version of yourself. Stand next to them so you are both facing in the same direction. Let them know that they will survive this moment. They will not only survive, but they will also thrive. They will live through this moment and grow to become the three-dimensional, multi-faceted and super-capable person you are now.

Take the younger version of yourself by the hand and change the surroundings in your visualisation.

You are now in a cinema with a big, white, empty screen in front of you. The lights go down. On the big screen will be the events of your life from that moment you found yourself up until now.

For this story to change the younger version of yourself, which still lives in your unconscious mind, they need to know that you lived through that traumatic moment you originally visualised. They need to see what you have become because of living through that moment. The person you are now would not exist without you living through that moment.

When you look at the younger version of yourself you will see a moment that they understand. Thank them for listening and let them go back into your unconscious mind facing that moment from your past with the knowledge that they will live and thrive.

Then break state. Have a dance or throw your arms around wildly and kick your legs out. Get some blood moving to change your physical state and bring you back, kinaesthetically into the world of now.

Notice how you now feel about this story. How do you now feel around taking action in the face of the story being changed?

When I first did this exercise around issues I was facing personally, it took me a good 3 times to really change the story I was telling myself. There was immediate change after doing it once. To keep it a long-term new story I then revisited it twice more.

Do this as many times as you need to change the story, or stories, you are telling yourself and staying stuck.

Make a list now of the stories you are telling yourself. Attend to them all and your achievements are potentially limitless.

Quieting the Mind

This hack will shortcut you to
a clean and clear mind

Have you ever found it difficult to sleep because your mind has been going around in circles around a problem or impending problem in your life?

Have you ever found it hard to concentrate, or hard to find the energy to take action due to all the "internal conversations" going on in your head?

Then this hack is for you.

I am going to teach you something that I learned from listening to a former military officer from the US's top military unit, the Delta Force.

Delta Force teach this technique to all their operatives because many days on active duty will begin with the soldier in question certain that they are unlikely to live through the day. The unit that went to arrest Osama Bin Laden was certain it was a suicide mission and that none of them would come back alive. They faced that fear and went.

The mission began with a 90-minute helicopter flight during which they could have had plenty of time to mull over their chances of survival, the likelihood it would go wrong and the chances that Bin Laden would blow himself and all of them to smithereens within the clothes he would be wearing.

Instead, they chose to have a sleep.

Can you imagine yourself sleeping under those circumstances? I find it difficult to imagine most of us being able to close our eyes and switch off with that level of certainty that we are about to die.

They used this technique to go straight to sleep. This meant they were fresh and alert when they landed out of the helicopter and into the mission.

Step 1 is to relax the muscles of the face. Release them completely and let them hang. Often vanity stops us doing this. We worry that people will think we look vacant if we let them see our faces without tension in them. Forget vanity. Release the muscles round the eyes, round the mouth, around the ears, along the jaw-line and let your face hang. As you proceed with the next step, let these muscles remain loose.

Step 2 is to move to the torso. Release the shoulders and neck muscles. Start with the cross where your shoulder muscles meet the spine then move to releasing the shoulders.

Move on to the arms, one at a time, and release the muscles in the arms so they sink.

Release the chest muscles and then the stomach muscles. Ask them to let go in your mind's eye. Move your way down the body asking each small bit of you to release, keeping everything released as you move down the body.

Once you have released the feet your breathing should be significantly slower.

Focus now on what is happening inside your head. Imagine a white sheet on a white background. Use this image to banish thoughts and images from your head. If an image comes into your mind, replace it immediately with this image.

If you hear your own voice in your head, start repeating the mantra "Stop thinking!" in your head. Repeat it over and over again, slowly and calmly.

Continue with this image and this mantra until you are asleep.

This is what is taught to all the military people who are promoted into the Delta Force. It works for them. Keep practising until this works for you.

Clearing your mind is central to being able to create a new narrative for your life. So many narratives exist in the world that are designed to stop you being successful. There are other narratives that are designed for you to be brilliant and successful. Learn how to tune the negative ones out. Learn how to recognise the narratives that will make your life, and the lives of those you love, better.

Chapter 8: Influence

The Difference Between Impact and Influence

What happens in the room, and
when you are not in the room

I'm guessing the title of this chapter has got your attention. After all, who does not want to be influential. At least, I imagine if you are reading this book, you would not want to be one of the people who is not influential.

Impact and influence are different things. I define them like this.

Impact is about what happens when you are in the room. Influence is about what happens when you are not in the room.

All the book up until this point has been about getting you in full command of your impact. Without that there can be no influence. Without knowing what your impact is (and being able to articulate your understanding of your impact) you are at the mercy of other peoples' interpretation of you and your behaviour.

You cannot be in the room all the time. Some conversations have to happen without you being there. After all, you can only be in one place at one time.

What would it be like to know that you have a presence in those rooms where you are not physically present?

What would it be like to be invited into conversations you feel excluded from at a higher management level?

What would it be like to be seen and heard as a valuable contributor or decision maker?

There are several questions to ask yourself here.

Are you aware of your value? Are you clear about what other people value about you in your current role? Do you know what the people who pay you value about you and your presence in the company?

What values do your management (or your customers if you run your own business) hold dear? How many of those values do those others not see in you yet?

Make a list of the values of your company and work out how many of them you espouse on a daily basis.

You might look at these questions and think to yourself – "I have no idea what people value about me!" Great. Now is the time to change that.

The only way to find out is to ask.

When a client is involved with my team and I, this is what we explore after we have got the presence voice and energy in the bag. Everything we have studied together so far has been about arming you with the skills and techniques you need to create an amazing impact in a room and real influence once you have left.

Now is the time to start asking. You can blame me. "I am reading this book on personal and professional development and the author suggests I ask these questions."

Ask the questions of your work colleagues, your clients, your staff (if you are the boss) and the management (if there are people above you in the management chain who pay you). The feedback from the people who pay you will be most instructive.

You are paid to the level of value that is perceived in relation to you and your presence in the company.

If we assume you are in employment for a few moments, then you can be sure that your bosses look down on you and think to themselves either: "How much do you cost me?" or "What a lot I get for my money." Do you remember we touched on this idea in an earlier chapter.

Which would you like them to be thinking about you? Are you clear what they are thinking about you? If the answer to the 2nd question is no, then this is where the work begins.

Who Fights Your Corner?

*You cannot make your dreams
happen on your own*

No one is an island.

Not a single human being on the planet has managed to create something worthwhile for themselves without the help and support of others.

The image of the self-made man, a heroic trope, just does not ring true in the real world. I remember one Sunday sitting in the auditorium of Excel, around 11 years ago, waiting for our headline speaker to arrive. Our headline speaker was Donald Trump. My sister and I had been at the Excel the whole time listening to speakers from 9am. At lunchtime the tannoy pumps out, "Mr Trump is in the UK!" "Oooh", gasps the 7000 present. At 4pm the tannoy calls out, "Mr Trump is in London!" "Aaaah!" gasps the throng of people. "Mr Trump is in the building!" at 5pm and so at 6pm Donald Trump takes to the stage to rapturous applause.

He then spends the 90-minute speech disparaging almost every single business associate he has ever worked with. He made it all happen himself. He fired his agent for doing a lousy job for him on The Apprentice. He fired this associate. He fired that deputy. They were useless.

It was a 90 minutes I did not expect. It was 180 degrees the opposite viewpoint of any of the other speakers that day.

It's totally untrue that Donald Trump made things happen

by himself. It may be a story he tells himself and believes himself. But it is not true.

We all need people who can speak for us when we are not in the room.

Who is speaking up for you when you are not in the room?

If the answer to that question is, "I don't know?" or "I don't think anyone is", then take stock and go back to the beginning of this book when I set the values exercise.

You need advocates. If you don't know who they are, or who they are going to be, then now is the time to start thinking strategically about how to find them and get them to go to work for you.

One of my advocates has been in my life for over 20 years now. We don't see each other often. We occasionally meet for lunch, or a Zoom chat. He is a man who contracted me with my first corporate client after seeing me in action delivering a presentation on the stage, on the hour, every hour for a full 8-hour day.

He has been in the background occasionally dropping me messages for the last 20 years, occasionally inviting me into meetings or for lunch with people he thinks may find me interesting. It is through this man that I found my first £50k client.

I know he speaks about me a lot when I am not in room. I know that I am often on his mind when he is engaged in exciting new projects.

Who, in your world, could be that kind of advocate for you?

Who has the ear of people who you would like to have your ear?

How many degrees of separation are there between you and the people who have real decision making about your career?

Here is a task for you to move this forward.

Think of 3 people in your organisation (or your network) who could make a big difference for you in your career. Whilst you are doing this exercise you may be tempted to think that the people you think of are unattainably far from you. Please do not censor who you have in mind.

Once you have found these 3 people, chart who they know who might be able to connect to you. If you cannot find anyone who can do that, then who do they know who knows someone. If you have to, then chart this back another degree of separation until you have someone who can introduce you to that someone who can introduce you to that someone until you get to the person you have chosen.

Think of this as a map to the treasure. If you want to find treasure on a desert island you need a map which tells you where the treasure is. You might have to climb this sand dune, or turn left at this palm tree, or swim under the waterfall or climb through the cave. Each of these milestones are the same as the people who you know chart as the guide to get you in front of the people you need to.

It is time to get strategic about your life and your network. Begin with this exercise and then follow the values work we do later in this chapter.

What Do the People You Report to Need to Experience?

*The secret of promotion is in the values
that you are not yet showing others*

When I have a client who is seeking a promotion, one of the first things we do is get them to go into their boss's office and ask for feedback around value.

The question that must be asked in this interview is this.

"If I come into this office in 6 months time and ask for a pay rise, what would you need to see and experience for it to be a no-brainer to say yes?"

This question elicits much clearer feedback than you would get otherwise.

If you ask people for feedback they will try and be helpful and tell you things like "You are really good". They have no reference point to give you feedback with any clarity. They will fob you off with their first thoughts.

If you give them a context in which to give you feedback then this gives them permission to give more honest feedback. If you want feedback on your presentation skills, no one will give you honest feedback unless you ask for specificity. "When you are watching me, please notice and give me feedback as to whether I am using the range of the voice or whether I sound monotonous." People need a point of focus. Give them a point of focus and they can be honest without feeling like they are being unpleasant to you. Ask blankly for "feedback" and people, in the main, are too scared to give you anything helpful. Granted, there are a small number of Cats who would happily tell you the truth at all times. Those Cats tend to live at the very top of the management tree.

It's likely you will have to interpret some of the responses you get from your boss. Recently a client of mine performed this task exactly as I write above. The response her boss gave her was "We need to see you burn less energy when we give you tasks." The phrase "burn less energy" is open to interpretation. She and I decided that it means revealing less negative emotion when in conversations about tasks that are proving tricky. Our focus has been on those conversations, and using the techniques shared in this book we have been transforming the way she is perceived inside the organisation and out. Although the promotion has not been offered, she has had, at the time of writing, 3 job offers from other similar companies all of whom buy into the value she potentially brings to their organisations.

Value is a perception. You cannot force value on people. You can represent a value in your physical presence, your tonal approach to others and in the language you use.

Often the values others want to see in us are values we would like others to see in us. Normally they are already inside us, just buried away somewhere inside.

Who here loves going to the movies? I certainly do. Have you ever sat watching a very exciting movie with an amazing hero (of any gender) stepping up and being brave, or physically accomplishing something astonishing? Whilst watching this hero in this movie, have you wished you were more like them?

Do you recognise that thought? If yes, then I have some good news for you.

We usually make mistakes in the way we interact with the images of our heroes. We think we are looking at something, a quality, we "wish" we had. Instead I would like to reframe that idea. We are really looking at a quality we already possess. We just don't yet know how to articulate this quality to the world. We watch our heroes intently in the hope they will show us how they do it.

Perhaps our heroes can be more useful to us if we can invite them into our homes.

I am not suggesting we invite them into our homes in real life. In many cases our heroes won't be able to articulate themselves in any useful way anyway.

We are going to tap into the power of the imagination.

You may have heard me say this before. The unconscious mind cannot tell the difference between that which is real and that which is imagined.

I'd like to show you here an exercise I get my clients to do in order they can be clearer about how to articulate more value.

At the beginning of this exercise I would like you to think of 3 values you would like people to experience or associate with you when you are in a room. This means that it may be useful for you to have done the previous exercise of tapping into what your boss (or your clients) do value in you. If you haven't done that, may I suggest you do before moving on to this exercise. After all, there is no point in working on a value people already see in you.

Write down your 3 values.

For each value I would like you to think of someone who represents that value for you. One person for each of the values.

Choose one of the values and the person who represents that value for you.

Imagine that person in the room you are in. Imagine them with clarity. Think of this image you are creating as the image on a television set. If the image is not clear, perhaps you want to use your internal remote to sharpen the picture up. If the image is too dull, perhaps you might want to turn up the brightness. If the image has no colour, perhaps press the colour button on your internal remote.

You decide when you have got this person in front of you with clarity. Look at them. Look at how they stand, look at how they hold themselves, how they dress and how they breathe. Get close to them. Your image is in 3 dimensions. Walk all around them. How is their eyeline?

When you feel you have gleaned enough information from walking around them, stand right behind them so your feet are lined up exactly one step behind them.

Take a breath and then move forward into their shoes. Step into that body you have been observing. Stand as they are standing, look through their eyes, breathe as they breathe. Stand inside that image for a minute until you feel what they are feeling in this moment.

When you have been inside that image of your hero for about a minute, or less if you feel the emotion abating, step back out and shake off the image and shake you body. It is important for you to do what we call "breaking state" at this point. Come back to you and your experience.

Write down everything you learned from standing inside that image of your hero.

When you are ready, move on to do the 2nd and then the 3rd.

Be More Valuable

*Where could your values intersect with
the values of your decision makers?*

When your bosses look down at the people they pay every month they look at you from a perspective of commodity or value. We have gone through this before.

Let me remind you because it is key to the topic in this sub-chapter.

In the commodity marketplace, "money" is the only consideration or topic. If you were to buy a book it would not matter where you bought it from because it would be the same book that arrives through your door. In that case, the price that various resellers offer the book at must be a major consideration. Amazon is helpful in that it, when it sells all of its produce, lists all the resellers for any item in order of price.

This means that employers look at the majority of their staff from a position of commodity. They look down at an individual employee and think to themselves, "How much do they cost me?" The presumption is that they see the person through the prism of their title, "salesperson", "director of HR", etc. The presumption is that the title can be filled by anyone who fits the criteria of the job. Someone is not that good, get someone else.

Alternatively the other market is the "value" marketplace. In the value marketplace price is not the major part of the conversation. The major part of the conversation is predicated on the idea of outcome. What is it they, or the company, gets because that person is in the job? When an employer is focused on the outcome, especially the tangible outcome, they receive from the individual, then they look down through the prism of the person rather than the title. The individual creates the outcome. When they look at the individual and think of the tangible outcome then the predominant thought is "Wow! What a lot I get for the money I pay this person."

To get you moving forward in your career we need your employers to be thinking about you in the 2nd way. The value space is always the one to pursue.

Back in 2011, when I worked with the Treasury Department of the RBS I was fired as I was passing through the revolving door out of their Liverpool Street office. This happened after a particularly difficult and unrewarding training session I completed with 6 senior members of staff.

3 months later I was rehired and the company was significantly slimmer in terms of the number of employees. They had made about a 1/3 of the staff redundant.

I had lunch with the financial director who had got me in to work with his staff. We sat in the canteen together and he explained to me why he had had me fired and then rehired. The reason, thankfully, had nothing to do with the quality of my work.

"We didn't want to waste money having you train people we were going to get rid of. Now we have culled (his word) 1/3 of the company, we were ready to get you back in."

Tough choices, right!

"How did you do that? What criteria did you use on who to get rid of?"

"Easy," he said to me. "We looked for everyone with their head down…and we fired them."

The presumption was that, unless you were making a special effort to create some sort of visibility around yourself, you were a commodity. Either you were irreplaceable, or redundant.

Sadly most people go through their working lives attempting to be invisible. Looking not to attract attention. It's another case of the hypothalamus associating visibility with the attraction of danger.

There is something in that. When you become visible it is usually because you take a stand about something. Taking a stand means risking enemies, or people who disagree with you being able to see and attack you.

This means that there can be no visibility without risk. It certainly means that there can be no visibility without stepping over fear. There can be no stepping over fear without honesty about your values.

Your values are the key to providing more value to the company.

If you have completed the values exercises in the previous part of this chapter you will have some idea of the values you want people to see. The question to ask now is, "How do these values intersect with the company's values?"*

Once you know the answer to this then it is time to work out who needs to see you in action revealing these values. Where do you need to be in order that you can show people the extra value you could bring them?

Extra value involves solving a bigger problem.

Decide for yourself what the bigger problem is that you would like to solve. Learn how to articulate your idea, create curiosity (so the Cats get curious in YOU) and take them on a journey as listeners. This means telling stories. It may also include telling stories about things that have yet to happen. When you tell stories about a future you can imagine, and you can do it in a way that they can imagine too, then be pleased. If they are running a movie in their mind's eye that involves working with you at a higher level, and it is working out well, then that makes the promotion so much easier.

If you are an entrepreneur reading this, then everything stands. Replace the word "boss" with the word "client" or "customer" and the principles of this chapter are the same.

If you want clients who will pay more money to you for a

---

* As a quick aside here, if your values and the company's do not intersect then you are in the wrong job. If you are a business owner and your values don't intersect with your customers/clients, then you need to change who you serve.

service, then find a bigger problem to solve than the one you are solving now. Find that and watch the turnover of your business rocket into the sky.

Reframing Perceptions

People put people in boxes because it's easier for them. Make it more difficult for them

Everyone puts people in boxes. Not literally. Human beings have to find shortcuts that make it easier to remember more people.

Have you heard of the Dunbar Number? The Dunbar number is named after Robin Dunbar, anthropologist, and evolutionary psychologist.

The Dunbar Number is 160.

Human beings used to live in caves in the Stone Age. When we lived in caves the average number of people in a tribe was 160. As the human brain was evolving it learned to cope with the number of names and faces that it would expect to meet in a lifetime. 160.

The human brain has not evolved (particularly) since then. We may think we are more sophisticated than the first people to discover language and communication. But we are not.

Now we live in the 21st Century where we are likely to meet more than 160 in a single day, if we live in a big city. The brain cannot cope. This is why, when we are in large crowds, we tend to put our eyes down toward the ground. Have you ever focused on your feet whilst walking down a busy street? I certainly have.

The hard drive of our brains can hold 160–200 (at most) names and faces and hold the context of how we know those people.

When we get past 200, we must delete someone to accommodate meeting new people.

Therefore, most of us will have the experience of seeing someone on the street who we know we know, but for the life of us, cannot remember where and how we know them. We once were able to do that, but our brain deleted them because we met someone new.

Let's take this information and turn it into something useful for you and your career.

If you can only hold 160–200 names, faces and context in your head, then the same holds true for any management above you.

It is imperative that you, your face and the context of knowing you, become one of those 160–200. The only way to do that is to become valuable to them.

First you must be seen. You have to be present in meetings. You must network. You need people talking about you and for you to be in charge of what it is they are saying.

If you do not, someone else will be. If someone else is, then the chances are you are the one who gets deleted from their brain. If you do, then they will look upon you as a commodity and therefore replaceable.

What People Need to Listen to You

*Decide who you need to be in front of
and how to get in front of them*

This is a simple part of the equation. It is time to make decisions.

You know that to progress you need the ear of other people. You need those ears to be the people who will make decisions about who is or isn't promoted. If you can't get to those people directly, then you need the ears of people who will be in meetings with and talk to those people, so they can deliver your message further up the management chain.

This may or may not include your immediate boss. Sometimes your immediate boss can be your ally. Sometimes they may not want to be an advocate for you. You have to work that out via your relationship with them.

A client of mine, Daphne, who worked in the compliance department of one of the world's biggest investment banks, had the challenge that her boss did not always play every card with a straight hand. Often what he said he would do inside the room was 180 degrees the opposite. He would offer support to my client when she was in the room and bad mouth her to others at his level when she wasn't present. She was very much the Cat, and he the Dog. As the Dog he would say whatever he felt he needed to in order that he stay in his post. He was fearful of Daphne's skill and credibility in her role and sought to undermine it at every opportunity.

For her, this was the challenge. How could she get past what this man was saying about her?

This is a global bank with offices in South Africa, Hong Kong, Singapore and the USA. This meant that they were all already delivering their major communications using Zoom and Skype. This was 2 years before the Pandemic and all attendant lockdowns.

We began by getting my client to suggest to some of the global leaders to come to a Zoom room with her to explore how she might be able to help them with the bigger challenges they faced. A few of them were pleased to be asked and agreed to do this. Daphne focused on the value she could offer. She came up with ideas as to how her department could be even more useful to the bank, and suggested ways that engagement with Compliance could save a bank facing millions of pounds worth of fines. To be clear, she never bad mouthed her boss or attempted anything that might be perceived as going behind his back.

In the Autumn of that year her boss moved on. The boss was replaced by a woman who had come to know of Daphne and her value. The new boss invited Daphne to be in her inner circle and proved to be a woman of substance. Daphne was on the promotion list.

Alternatively you may want to see what you can do to change your boss's perception of you.

Alan, a client of mine in Switzerland, was in a deputy head position within a large Swiss insurance company. Alan was miserable in his job when we first met. "Get me out of here" he begged me during our first meeting.

Alan's issue was that his boss just "did not get him at all". Alan hailed from the US. His boss hailed from the German end of Switzerland. One was bright, cheerful and gregarious. The other, quiet, reflective and taciturn.

Alan and I did a few exercises together that revealed what Alan felt his boss needed to see and experience. Alan wanted his boss to see him as someone credible. Alan chose to adapt and give the boss what he needed. The result was that 4 months later that boss promoted Alan and gave him his own department to run. Alan was now super happy and excited about the possibilities ahead in his new role.

What matters now is that you know who it is in your world who needs to see the new you, the one that stands for the values you want them to see. Choose 3 people at least who need to see this and work out ways to meet them. Networking is a great way to do this. Where are they networking? By the way, if you don't think they are, you are wrong. Every successful person has a network to call on. The idea of self-made is nonsense. Invite them to meet you. Offer to be of service. Let them know how you might help solve the bigger problem.

Once you have started on this course, it will get easier. Stay with it and you will be rewarded.

Chapter 9: Money and You

What Do You Think Money Is?

Money is not what you think it is

In this chapter we come to the most divisive topic of all. More than any other topic in the world, conversation about money stirs up all sort of feelings. As a species we are happier to reveal the innermost workings of our personal relationships – spectacular failures and all – rather than reveal to a friend or family member what we earn.

Here is an exercise for you to do before moving on to the next part of this chapter.

Find a piece of paper. Do this exercise on paper with a pen or pencil. The act of writing will connect you more deeply to your emotions. The more physical action you take the deeper you go.

Write a list. On that list put everything that you think money is or means to you. Also write down what it would mean if you had enough money, or certainly more money than you have now.

Compare your list with some of the things that I and many of my colleagues and clients have put down when we were asked to do this exercise.

Money is:

- Security
- Success
- Dirty

- A burden
- Scarce
- Scary
- Mine
- The Root of All Evil
- Someone Else's

If I had money it would mean:

- I am greedy
- I am a bad person
- I should hide it from others
- I would be a better person
- I would get recognition
- I would be valuable
- I'd become a bad person

There are many, many more that I have seen written down or expressed by people seeking to change their circumstances and their lives.

Men and women have different attitudes to money too.

In the average law firm, every male lawyer is likely to walk into their boss's office and utter the words "Pay me more" to their boss. They may get a yes or a no, either way they leave the office having asked, being secure in their value to their firm.

Most female lawyers will not do the same. If asked they will most often say, "I couldn't do that."

This is a huge part of why there is an enormous aggregate disparity between male and female pay.

Social science tells us that men are more likely to chase money for the sake of money. It also tells us that women are unlikely to connect to the idea of money unless it is connected to a thing of value to them. For instance, if I had more money, I could have a house in this area or if I had more money, I could achieve this for myself or my family.

This statement is, of course, a generalisation. It is a generalisation that comes from a multitude of sources in social science.

Now here is the bare truth.

What is money and what does it mean?

Money is…

- Paper and metal coins.

That's it. That is all money is.

Ok, maybe money is also in the 21st Century, 0s and 1s in a computer system. In fact more and more money becomes virtual. Many of the biggest financial transfers that happen in the world today are done by a computer terminal talking to another computer terminal. No real hard paper cash changes hands.

I reiterate. That is it. That is all money is. Everything else you listed around the idea of money is in your head. We all tell ourselves stories around money and what it means. For many of us, the stories are what prevents us having what we really value in our lives.

In this chapter we are going to explore the ideas around the stories we tell ourselves around money and what we can do to change that experience for us.

By the way, the idea (and the feeling) of scarcity around money can happen to any of us, regardless of where we sit in the financial hierarchy of this country, or this world.

The current (at the time of writing this) Prime Minister in the UK, Boris Johnson, has spoken out about how the wage he earns as Prime Minister of the country, in 2021, is approximately £161k. Yet he is of the belief that he is being bankrupted by how little he is earning doing this job.

Some of the clients I have worked with who come to me with the highest wages already coming in have got a broken money mindset. As a result, their experience of what they are earning is somewhat less than satisfying.

All of us need to work on our money mindset. Even me. We will all have what we call "set points" around money that will trigger the stories and stop us from moving forward toward the goal.

A "set point" is when we consider a financial sum something that would be difficult for us to reach. For many of us the set point is around the potential of what we could earn if we were promoted.

We work on our money mindset, pass the set point and congratulate ourselves on our skill making that happen.

Here comes the next set point. The next financial hurdle. When we reach the next hurdle the same stories come back to haunt us and we have to work on our mindset again.

Should You Have Money?

82 Trillion Dollars are exchanged every day, on average, around the world

"I'm not the sort of person who gets money."

I have heard this story told many times by people in my extended family. I also remember my old friends from the world of theatre trying to save me from my "greed" when I started telling them how much money I was earning as a coach.

The theatre is a landscape with some of the most broken money mindsets I have ever seen. In the theatre it is quite normal to subsidise your industry by working for free. Actors will work for no money in the vaguest of hopes that doing so might result in getting paid the measliest of sums. Jealousy and scarcity run rampant in this world. It is the only industry I can think of where people in the industry will pay a lot of money to go to a play (and theatre is expensive to see from a penniless actor's perspective), to watch another actor play the part they did not get in the audition. That actor will spend the entirety of the play watching that actor and thinking to themselves "I could have done that better." I plead guilty. I did this many times during my life in this community. I did it because it was the norm in this community.

Imagine that was you living in that community and having that mindset around money. Can you imagine how much scarcity I must have believed in at that time of my life?

Another community who I regularly serve is health and wellness practitioners. I am talking about osteopaths, massage therapists, physiotherapists and talking therapy practitioners. Most of these people come from a place of giving. Their desire is to serve, to enrich the lives of others. Their emotional commitment to giving means they often give for free, little realising they undermine the quality of their own skills, exhausting themselves with no (or little) reward. They then compare themselves to others, assuming a scarcity of audience, and if they charge money, go cheaper in order they can have access to the little audience there is.

For many of these communities believe that there is a finite amount of money in the world, therefore a finite number of people who can have access to that money.

The truth is somewhat different.

The average amount of money that is moved between people in the world is 82 Trillion Dollars per day. Per Day! That is 12 zeros following the 82.

$82, 000, 000, 000, 000

Per Day!

Can you imagine such a figure in cash?

Now ask yourself this – Is there a good reason why a tiny portion of this money should not stop by you for a while?

Even if all you wanted is 0.001% of that then you still have $82, 000, 000, 000.

Per Day!

I am going to reiterate it until it goes in.

This is the amount of money that is exchanged between human beings on a daily basis.

Please give me a good reason why a tiny bit of that should not stop by you.

The job now is to find out where the money is and stand in its way until a little of it stops with you.

Knowing this, how does this change how you feel about asking for a pay rise. Asking for a pay rise today.

The flip side of this is that governments keep printing more money to get themselves out of the messes that they create economically that affect us all.

Every time they do this the value of the $82, 000, 000, 000, 000 lessens. Another reason to ask for the pay rise today.

Or, if the thought of that is too scary for today, to go in and ask your boss, "What do you need to see from me so that when I ask for a pay rise in 6 months, it is a no-brainer to say yes?"

Getting paid more is always about value. If you are clear as to what value you deliver, getting the money deserved is easier.

Stories Regarding Money

*What stories are you telling
yourself about money?*

When my children were younger, we spent a lot of time at the local sports centre, where my wife worked, in Hampshire. Often on a Saturday morning I would take them both to the sports centre ball park and let them play whilst I took my laptop and did some work.

I remember the conversation turning one Saturday morning, as I sipped the not-especially-good coffee. My daughter was 8 at the time. She posited to me that she didn't want to have lots of money when she grew up.

- "Hmmm," I pondered, "How come?"
- "Oh," she said to me. "If I had lots of money it would mean I would be a greedy and selfish person."
- "Ah," said I in my best coaching voice. "Did you know that money only exacerbates who and what you already are."
- "Mum," screams my daughter, at the top of her voice. "Dad says I am greedy and selfish."

I began to do some detective work in my head.

Where did she get that idea from? The idea that having money would mean she would be changed as a person.

She got it from stories told through the generations down the family line.*

In my own family there were many stories about making safe and secure choices. My parents saved the majority of their adult lives and left an amazing legacy that enabled me to own my first property. They never spent money on things they considered waste.

My parents were pretty atypical of the usual Scottish middle-class family. They were true blue Conservatives, a rarity even in the 1980s in Scotland. They taught me a work ethic because they themselves had had to work hard. Both my father and mother grew up in substantially poorer households than the one I grew up in. My parents were children just prior to and during the 2nd World War.

---

* Now that she is older, she is in possession of Robert Kiyosaki's *Rich Dad, Poor Dad* book and has a better understanding of money. She also, at the age of 13, won a job in a local boutique café and has become invaluable to Cherry, the lady who owns the coffee shop. Many of her school friends are jealous and seek to undermine her confidence around her having the job.

My father grew up in an army household. My mother, the daughter of a shop steward in a timber plant near Dundee.

Both devoted themselves to the idea of saving because they never wanted the level of difficulty and poverty they experienced to be visited on me and my sister.

They sent us to 2 of the finest fee paying schools in Edinburgh. They were selfless to a T. Even in his old age my father never was frivolous with money. Their intent was always to transfer it over to my sister and I in a way that set us up forever. My own financial adviser refers to me as a "trust baby".

The stories that had been passed down through the generations were around attracting attention. Keep your head down and don't attract attention was the key to success, was the story. Keep everything you can, sacrifice your own pleasures.

My parents were hardly the Presbyterian killjoys you often hear of in relation to Scotland. They had a great life together, visited many exciting and lush places around the world and were extremely comfortable. My love of good food and wine comes from them.

I now make my living out of attracting attention. I always did really, even in the theatre. Although they supported me in a theatre career, and financially too, they did not understand the world. Like I said earlier, the acting fraternity have, collectively, the worst mindset around money in the world.

Think about the stories that actors and artists tell themselves in order to justify their persistence through penury. To be struggling or starving in the artistic world is to be "virtuous" and "romantic". Think of how many films there are, especially from Hollywood, that romanticise the idea of being poor. How many romantic comedies revolve around a rich person falling in love with a poor person and running away to a wonderful, happy life of poverty. How many heroines in films and books are bound by marriage to someone who is rich, but cold and heartless? Look at a film like *Titanic* that spends a deal of time admiring and lionizing the emotional life of the passengers in 3rd class; drinking freely, loving freely, dancing with freedom. The other side of the equation is the passengers in 1st class. Cold, heartless, cruel, lying to each other and themselves. Is there any wonder that stereotypes around the idea of what it means to be wealthy are disseminated through popular culture so often and so readily.

Interesting isn't it, that the big money that is Hollywood likes to permeate the "old stories" to keep people in a state of poverty, the romanticism of it. It is almost as if they themselves were bound by a feeling of scarcity. There is a fear that if the poor find out how to make money that they themselves may be deposed and no longer able to earn themselves. Give them bread and circuses. Nothing has changed since Roman times in that respect.

My wife's family had a story. "We always made sure as soon as money came into the house we would send it back out again as quickly as we can." This sentence I have heard many times told round the dinner table. What a terrible evil money must be to be got rid of so quickly.

Even in the highest financial levels there is a guilt. There is a financial securities company I am working with right now. The client, who emailed me recently saying, "I've got the budget. Let's get going", would not talk to me about payment. My response to him, after talking over what he wanted to achieve, was "Who should I address the invoice to? Are you happy for me to invoice the entire investment?"

"Oh, I don't talk about money", he said. "You have to talk with invoicing about money." There was a disdain around the idea. Talking about money is tasteless and trite. We don't do it here in this office.

Yet money is the currency of the entire business.

You don't have a business unless there is money in the bank. If you don't have it, you have an idea, not a business.

If you don't get paid regularly you do not have a career. You have an expensive hobby.

I'd love it if you would take time now, before moving further, to spend time with the people in your life who matter the most. Perhaps a partner, perhaps children, perhaps close friends. Take an hour to talk about money. See and feel the emotions that come into the room. Explore with your family what the stories are around money you were told through childhood. How have you assimilated those stories into your life? What can you do now to let those stories go and create a different, and better result?

The 3 Chair Exercise

An exercise that will transform your
relationship with money and yourself

What can you do to let these stories go?

Do you want to let them go and create your own story about money?

If you do, it is going to take some bravery on your part.

I am going to recommend you get to know money better. We are going to do an exercise that will connect you with your unconscious mind and show you what stories are in charge there.

It is called the 3 Chair Exercise.

This is because the exercise involves 3 chairs. Find yourself a room with 3 chairs in it. This must be somewhere you will be free and open to express yourself whatever comes up for you when you do this. I have observed many clients have extreme emotional events doing this exercise. You do not want to feel that you must censor yourself when doing this.

Place the 3 chairs so that 2 are facing each other and the 3rd is in a triangular position. From the 3rd seat you will be able to observe what is happening in the 2 other chairs. Give yourself some space to move around the chairs.

As always this exercise involves exercising the imagination.

It's important that you have some money with you to do this exercise. It is preferable to carry cash and the largest denomination you can find. If it involves withdrawing money from a cashpoint then it is worth doing so. The higher level of money we use in the exercise the closer we will come to exploring what is really going on about money for you.

If it is not possible to use cash then a debit or credit card will work, though it lacks the same visceral quality that cash does.

Take your place in the 1st chair and place the money on the 2nd. Take a moment to look at your money. Open your imagination. What do you see in the chair? What does money mean to you? Let an image form in your mind. In my experience of doing this exercise I have heard people tell me of the most wildly different images coming to them. For one – a treasure chest with no key. For another – a large mound of cash surrounded by a ring of fire. For a third – a person looking back at them. Whatever you visualise is absolutely fine. It is your imagination at work.

By doing this we are tapping into the unconscious mind where the real damage can be done that keeps us from having the money we want.

Take time to let the image form. Sometimes it comes immediately, sometimes it takes time. Keep breathing into this. Do this at a time that you feel relaxed, not pressured.

Perhaps if you are not primarily a visual thinker what may come to you is a feeling or a sound. Whatever comes is what you need.

Imagine that you have a remote control with you, like the remote for a television. If the image isn't clear enough then use the remote to focus the image into sharp clarity.

Perhaps the image is in black and white, or the colours are muted. It's possible you are happy with that. It is also possible that by turning the colour up on your remote it might make the image feel more real to you.

Maybe you need to make the image larger in the chair opposite.

Could you reach out and touch it? Does it feel near or far away? Reach forward from the 1st chair and see if you can touch it or not.

Note every aspect of this. There is no right or wrong here. Only information that helps you transform your relationship with money.

What would you like to say to money? It can be anything. As before, I have heard many responses from people who want to communicate with money.

- "Why is it so difficult to keep you?"
- "I want more of you in my life."
- "I'm so angry with you, money."

The above quotes cover only a small percentage of the many responses I have guided my clients through with this exercise. Nothing is off limits in your response.

Once you have said everything you want to say to money then release and experience the feeling you have letting that out of your system.

In a moment you are going to stand up. When you stand you will leave an image of you in the chair.

When ready, stand up from your chair and shake your body out. Perhaps you might like to use the shaking out "energy" exercise from one of the previous chapters. It is important to break state here so you can go into the next part of the exercise without the hangover of your experience in the 1st chair. The feelings you experienced in the chair should remain with the image of you left there.

When you feel you are emotionally neutral and relaxed enough to move forward you are going to take your place on the 2nd chair on top of the money you put there. Yes, that is right. You are going to sit on your money. As you do so you will become money.

Don't ask me why this works. It just does. You become money.

As you sit in the 2nd chair, as money, look back at yourself in the 1st chair (where you left your image). As money, what do you want to tell the self in the other chair?

This is where we find the real intentions of money. Money is an energy, and it is mostly a benign energy. Many of my clients find it a shock to discover that money has a benign nature and wishes the best for them.

For most people doing this exercise, whatever money says back to them is a revelation. I'm not going to deliver quotes here. I don't want to lead you (or lead money) in its response to you.

Whatever money wants to say to you, let it say it.

When you are done, stand up again and shake out whatever energy you had in the chair. Shake it until you feel neutral because in a moment you are going to sit in the 3rd chair.

In the 3rd chair you will become the observer. The observer is a neutral position that can see both "you" in the 1st chair and money in the 2nd. The observer observes you and money interacting.

Sit now in the 3rd chair as the observer and look at the images in the 1st and 2nd chairs. What do you notice observing them both? Do they need to sit closer to each other? Further away? What do you notice about your posture in chair 1 as you connect with money?

Write down your observations so you can refer to them later. Stand up from the 3rd chair when you feel you have seen everything there is to see here. Shake it off in the usual manner.

Now we will go back to the 1st chair, and you will sit down into the image of yourself there. Now you are the new you. You are the "you" that now has the knowledge and the intelligence of sitting in all of the 3 chair positions. You are aware of all perceptual positions in this topic.

Look back at money in the 2nd chair. What do you want to say to money now you have this new insight? Say it out loud. Let money hear it.

When you have finished speaking to money, take a moment. Imagine there is a 4th chair sitting next to you in the 1st.

Most of us have retained a money mindset and a story around money that comes from our parents.

The question to ask now is this. If you could ask your mother or your father to step up and sit in the 4th chair next to you, who would you choose? Choose the first thing that comes to you, even if it makes no logical sense. Invite their image to come to you and sit next to you.

- Look at your parent in the 4th chair and say this to them. You may want to say this a few times.
- "With love and respect, I return this story about money to you. It is yours and not mine. Thank you for the love you gave it to me with. I now return it. I no longer need it."
- When you are done, stand up and shake it all off for the last time.
- The exercise is now finished.

I cannot tell you what experience you will have when doing this exercise. I can tell you that many of my clients have experienced the most intense emotional feeling during this. Many of them leave the exercise feeling a massive weight lifted or a sense of purpose around earning more money that they have never had before. Whatever you feel is exactly what you need to feel. There is no right or wrong. This is your experience and no one else's.

Some of my clients have done this exercise on a daily basis for a period of a week, a fortnight or a month. They make it a "must" in their lives because they recognise the value of connecting themselves with these feelings and ridding themselves of stories that don't belong to them. The images will change as you do this. What money is in the seat opposite may change daily. Whatever you see is your unconscious mind talking directly to you.

I wish you all the best with this.

Visualising What You Want

*Nothing will come to you unless you
fix it, with specificity, in your mind*

Earlier in this chapter I said that most women find it difficult
to focus on the idea of money just for the sake of money. This
is also true of many men. It is the rare super-Alpha males who
can focus on the image of money and chase it for its own sake.

The rest of us need to have a reason to want it in our lives.
We all need a purpose in life, otherwise we will never move
forward. We need a desire. We need something we desire
enough to be uncomfortable. We need something we desire
enough to get up in the morning and make an effort to do
something different.

Recently I was at a party, a birthday party for a friend of
my wife.

This lady has mostly everything she would wish for. Her
husband earns amazing money. She has a beautiful car. She
has a beautiful house. She has no job or interest beyond shop-
ping, meeting friends and drinking and eating.

The party was full of people who had the same experience.
Money was easy to come by. It had been a while since I had
been to a party where the conversation remained very much
on the surface. In fact, my alarm bells began to ring when the
main topic of conversation, whichever group I joined in with,
was around how drunk we all were last time we got together
and "Wasn't that the worst hangover you ever had!?"

It wasn't long before most of the people around me were
super sloshed in alcohol and making very little sense. It was
less than an hour after that I saw that drugs were being taken
openly in the living room of the party.

You might be reading this and thinking "that David is a bit
of a prude. Has he never enjoyed himself?" The answer is yes,
I know how to enjoy myself and have fun. I am rather partial

to a glass of champagne. However, I have no relationship with the reality of life that demands I do my best to escape it. This was not a house full of teenagers. This was a house full of supposedly responsible adults in their 40s and 50s.

Watching this it became really clear to me that my wife and I were the only people at this party who did not despise their lives and the choices they had made. Not only that, I was observing the behaviour of people who had given up. They had no purpose.

In *Alice in Wonderland*, there is a moment when Alice meets the Cheshire Cat.

- "Which way should I go?" she enquires of the Cheshire Cat.
- "Where do you want to get to?" he retorts.
- "I have no idea" she responds.
- "Well then, why would it matter which way you go?"

I paraphrase, and mainly from my memory of the animated Disney version.

Think about this. All knowledge available to humanity is available free and online. At the resource we know as "YouTube" there are videos on almost every possible subject including how to get super wealthy and how to be super fit. Would you agree those 2 categories would be pretty popular? All the knowledge any of us need is out there, free, and open to find.

So how come so few of us are millionaires with 6-packs?

For most of us the answer is because we are not motivated enough to do something about it. The reason we are not motivated is that we are not in touch with the life we want to have. If you are not in touch with what you want in life, then how can you possibly know what to do and where to put the effort?

Being clear about what you want and who you want to become whilst pursuing it is the key to motivating yourself into action. If a desire is strong enough, it will sustain you when you wake up not in the mood, when life hits you with something awful that makes you want to give up and when people in your community start to tell you "it's not worth trying".

For instance, where do you want to be living in the world in 5 years time? If you could choose anywhere in the world, where would it be?

Most of us are afraid to dream. Think about how you responded to my question above. What did you immediately think of? Was it a home somewhere near where you live now? Was it a dream that was relatively conservative?

Be precise about what you want to create. Visualise it. Put imaginary movie screens on your wall and imagine in detail where you would live if you could live anywhere in the world. Imagine a home in detail. Imagine the intricacy of the brickwork. Imagine the front door. What colour is your front door?

I'm guessing the house you are imagining is somewhat more expensive that the house you live in now. Owning this house will require you to be earning significantly more than you do now.

Once you know the answer to all the questions around the life you want to have, then visualise it every day. Once you have imagined the movie in your head, imagine it every day. Imagine it clearly. Make sure the focus of the movie is UHD crystal sharp. Look at it in extreme close up in your mind. See yourself in it.

Connect with this regularly. Preferably do it daily. This will give you the motivation to take action. Taking action is the only thing that will make this goal a reality. This goal will help define what the right action is for you to receive the kind of income that means having this home (or whatever really matters to you in life) is going to happen.

Who Do You Have to Become to Earn?

*You are either bigger than your
circumstances, or you are not. Which is it?*

"For the journey" used to be the tag line for Lloyds Bank in a series of commercials they recently ran in the UK.

We know that knowledge by itself doesn't provoke any action. We know that motivation lasts almost as long as soap does in a bath.

As long as human beings are growing they can feel satisfaction in life. Remember that in the plant world you are either growing or dying. There is no such thing as stasis. The idea of stasis is a human lie. We lie to ourselves constantly. We lie in the idea that we stay the same. Many do try. Many escape this truth via drink, drugs, gambling, and all sorts of other things in which we immerse ourselves in order not to face up to the truth. The people at that party I talked about were most definitely in that place.

In the previous section we focused on what it is you want to create for yourself. In this section we are going to focus on who you need to become to make that a reality.

Tony Robbins famously said, "See things as they really are, not worse, not better".

I'm sure that isn't the first time you heard this in this book. It's a basic tenet of making things change in your life.

You have a choice. All of us have difficult circumstances in our lives. Some more than others. Some now more than last month, some less than last month.

We all face the choice of deciding whether to be bigger than our circumstances or not. We all make a choice as to whether to be resourceful or not. Sometimes we choose the quiet life. Even though we live in the 21st Century it is still sadly the case that many women still allow their husbands to define what they can create. Often the quiet life is not as quiet as it would appear to be.

Only recently I had a client, a woman in the world of health and wellness, who came to me and decided to invest, sending me over a deposit for a programme of work together. I was super excited for her because I knew that what we could create together for her, and her children, was massive.

The next day she sent me an email demanding a refund and that I not make contact. It seemed odd in relation to the conversation that we had the day before. I emailed her first to say that I would be open to discussing a refund and stopping our professional relationship and that it was company policy to discuss on a call.

When I rang her, I was speaking to the same person, yet a very different person to the one I spoke to a day ago. It became apparent quickly that her husband was now on the call with us, listening in. I could hear him in the background repeating over again, "Get the money back! Get the money back!" The person I was talking to the day before was gone. The person in front of me now is the face she plays when her husband is in the room. It wasn't the authentic face for this woman. It was heart-breaking to hear.

She subtly intimated that if I didn't return the money fully then it would leave her in a "difficult domestic situation". How might you interpret that remark? I took it to mean that there might be intimidation and potentially abuse that she would be subject to. I returned the money.

It truly was a heart-breaking situation. She said herself she had to make a choice. Her own needs or her husband's. She chose her husband. She may be under the impression she has chosen the quiet life in doing so. However, nothing could be further from the truth.

The truth is that a can has been kicked down the road. She chose not to be bigger than her circumstances here.* How-

---

* To be clear I have the greatest respect and empathy for whatever that prospective client was going through and would never, ever want to indirectly be responsible for someone vulnerable being

ever, she is subsuming herself inside someone else's definition of her and that is not sustainable. At some point this will
break down for her, which is why I have kept the door open
for her return when she is ready.

Your current circumstances may not be as extreme as that.
Whether they are or are not, recognise that you are making
choices, even if you are avoiding making choices. Avoiding
making a choice is allowing others to make choices for you.
That means that others' pleasure and satisfaction are more
important than your own. Staying in a world where you must
subsume who you are is a choice.

Think back now to the goals you decided you want and are
now visualising regularly. Whilst you are visualising those
goals see a picture of yourself in the future enjoying those
goals. Who is this person? Who is she now? How does she
differ from you now having this vision? What does she possess that you do not? Visualise this person with detail. I want
you to be really clear about who you must become in order
to attain the goal.

Once you have this clarity on what you want and who you
need to become, your action plan will appear for you. You
will know what action steps will make this person and this
result happen. You will be clear about the order of the action
steps. You will be clear about the timeframe in which you can
become this new, better version of yourself.

Become this person and operate fully and freely as this
person and the goal you want to achieve will be given to you
by the universe.

To be clear, I am not suggesting that it is going to be easy.
Nothing worthwhile in life comes easily. Becoming a better

---

on the end of violence, as I considered implied by her statement.
However, ultimately the person in question makes a decision
around what they are willing to accept in their life. I cannot want
them to be free more than they do. It will backfire. Which is why I
returned the money and left the door open for her to approach me
if she ever decides to take charge for herself.

version of yourself is difficult. It requires work. What work there is, is up to you. It all becomes clear when you confront who you are and who you would rather be. Embrace it, love who you are now and love who you are going to become even more.

Isn't it interesting that this chapter, ostensibly about money, is about so much internal stuff? Our experience of the world and our attitudes and ideas around money are all connected with the inner workings of the unconscious mind. To clear stuff out and emerge stronger, and wealthier financially, we have to work on ourselves and change the stories in our minds.

Chapter 10: Creating Advocacy

How You Can Help

Begin with Palm Down Networking

No one can make it on their own. The idea of the "self-made man" is a myth. As much as successful men love to disseminate the story of how they heroically made it to the top by themselves, it is never the case that this is true.

This is something I didn't know when I was an actor and director. I thought it was all about working hard and so I did. I would make it myself. I never asked for help. I never asked for favours.

That is my disadvantage as a man.

Everyone needs advocacy in their lives. Advocacy is other people who are in a position to help choosing to help, you because they recognise in you something of value.

This means having a supportive network. This means being connected to people who operate in the spheres you want to operate in (rather than the ones you operate in now).

This means having a strategy around how, where and with whom you are networking.

So where are you networking right now? Who are you networking with in your organisation? If you run your own business, are you networking where your clients might be? Or are you networking where people are who can feed you your clients?

Ladies who are reading this, I have some excellent news for you. You are much better at connecting with people than men are. You are much better at feeling the emotional signals given by others. You are much better at making relationship something more than transactional.

Every one of my clients who have made advances in their careers or business did so because they had other people advocating for them when they were not in the room. To get more clients in a business, then the quickest way to increase your turnover is to get your clients talking about you to their network and friends.

If you are in a job and your desire is promotion then people above you in the management chain must have their eyes and ears on you, or if that is not possible, they must have their eyes and ears on people who will talk about you and how valuable you are.

What better way of signalling your value than to help others?

If you are unsure where to begin, find out now. Where do the people above you in the management chain hang out? Where do they network with each other? What meeting opportunities are there for you to attend or offer to host or facilitate?

A client of mine, Clare, was in the same job for 21 years, with one of the major banks. Until we started working together she had never thought about her career, working on working harder and being very good at her job. At 21 years she had to admit that she was really quite bored with doing the same thing, even though she did it well. Thinking about her career in different terms, she began working with me because she was interested in presenting well. It was around 2 months into the engagement that she was promoted out of the old job and into some new responsibilities. She said she had used the techniques to interview well and had put her name up for things without considering that she would be seen. This is all well and good. Unfortunately the new job did not involve Clare getting any extra money. Hmmm, I can't leave it there then, can I?

Recent developments as she becomes more confident in her visibility include being asked to be on panels of experts on specific parts of the business as well as recording several video pieces for the bank's internal intranet. She is volunteering to run a series of podcasts around an event the bank runs every 3 months (I call it Clare FM) which will give her even more visibility. She will be recording her videos and speaking on the panels next month. I tasked her earlier today to create a list of people, above her in the management chain, who she would like to be networking with, and work out ways to make sure they know she is on these panels and that these videos exist.

The focus of any action should be "giving". This is what I call palm down networking. In palm down networking you go networking with a giving hand rather than a begging hand.

Remember the Zig Ziglar quote, "You can have anything you want as long as you help enough other people have what they want first."

Think about those around you and above you in your organisation. Choose 5 or 6 people whose ear you would like to have access to. Note them down on a piece of paper. Then work out where they network and work out how you can get invited there.

Getting Great Results Quickly

It is all in the system. Know what to do first

Once you get in front of the people you want to be in front of then you must work out what it is you are going to say. This is where most people fall down. They fall down because they haven't worked this out in advance. They get the opportunity and then freeze when the person they meet sets eyes on them and says "Hello".

We need to follow the systems for networking.

There are 3 basic elements to the system for networking:

1. Preparation
2. Attending
3. Following Up.

Preparation involves making sure that you know everything you need to know about the network you plan to attend. Networking is you working on your career rather than in your job. We often sacrifice our time toward the job and make networking of secondary importance. That's a mistake. It tells us we value our own lives less than we value those we work for.

Do you know where this network will be held? Is it virtual or face to face? What time does it start? What time does it end? How long do I need to set aside to get there? How much extra time should I put aside for connecting after the event is over? What do I wear?

Do you need business cards? Yes. Do I give out my business cards to everyone? No. You don't want to look desperate. Business cards typically go in the bin after networking, so never give it out unless you have a very good reason, and preferably only when someone else gives you their business card at the same time.

The 2nd step is attending. Without attending you have no visibility.

Once there you want to live by the maxim of palm down networking.

Palm down networking is about seizing the opportunity to be of more value.

You need to know how to articulate your value to the organisation you work for especially as the question you are most often going to be asked when you meet new people is, "And what do you do?"

We do this not through our title. To use your title com-moditises you.

We use the following. We articulate 3 elements of value that we deliver in our work.

Those 3 elements are:

- The People Who benefit
- The Problem They Face
- The Solution You (and your team if appropriate) Give Them

In the entrepreneur world this is called an "audio-logo" or "audio-billboard". Both of those terms are marketing speak that suggest that articulating your value this way is similar to stopping by a big billboard at the side of the road. Either what you see on the billboard stays with you or it doesn't. Have you ever had that experience? You're sitting in your car at a set of traffic lights. You look up and see a billboard for the latest hit TV series on Netflix, or Disney, or Amazon. What you see creates curiosity or it doesn't (because you are not the right audience). If it does resonate then you make a mental note to check your Netflix account and put a note on to watch it later.

Will what you say make people you meet make a mental note about you to check you out later?

Giving First

Be a person of integrity, so they
see a person of integrity

Having articulated yourself in a way that creates curiosity around your value, we now look to how you can provide more value to the people you meet.

We are palm down networking. Palm down networking focuses on a giving hand.

When we meet people whilst networking, we want to get the articulation of our own value done so we can enter into a deeper conversation.

Ask lots of questions. We want to find out what their challenges are. As we talk about the problem that we solve in our roles, we want to focus on the problems they solve in their role and the challenges they are facing now. The conversation may only be about work, or it may be appropriate to stray outside of the topic of work.

Always FORD ahead in your networking.

The acronym FORD stands for 4 things that every human being has in this world:

- F – Family
- O – Occupation
- R – Recreation
- D – Dreams

There are 4 levels at which you can connect with and build rapport quickly in any networking situation. Usually, we start with Occupation as it is the safest topic to tackle. If you stick to that being the only topic of conversation then you risk being placed, by the listener, in the commodity space. The more you can get someone to reveal of themselves the more rounded a human being they will be to you, the more they feel listened to and the safer they will feel.

In this book we have concentrated on helping you understand and action techniques that will help others feel safe in your company. One thing is for sure, if you don't make people feel safe, it is unlikely that they will "open up" to you. Now is the time to play to the strengths of everything we have advised in the previous chapters. Networking well opens up many avenues of potential success for anyone who uses these techniques.

Little things make a difference. A client of mine once found themselves a great advocate. When they met them whilst networking they asked them about what challenges they were facing in their lives right now. The person they were talking to said "Nothing, really" at first, but after spending a little time finding out more about them personally they said "I could really do with someone clearing out my garage. I keep trying to find the time to do but it never happens." My client found them a younger member of their own family who, for a small payment (which they were very pleased to receive) the challenge was solved. A little thing, perhaps. That little thing meant my client had the ear of someone who was extremely grateful. The relationship has been developing ever since.

Integrity is a word often bandied about and very rarely understood.

Integrity means being a person of your word. If you say you are going to do something, then do it. That is the simple definition of integrity. This brings us to the 3rd element of successful networking, Follow Up.

Never say you are going to do something for someone unless you have the intention to make it happen, then make sure it happens.

Therefore, you never give your business card to people unless they give theirs to you. When you hand over your business card you are giving a bit of power over to the other person unless the exchange is mutual. You need their business card more than they need yours, especially if you have made a promise to them.

Take charge of whatever the next step is going to be. Perhaps you have someone to introduce to them from your own network. Lay it out clearly what you intend to do.

"Thanks for your business card. I intend to call you tomorrow and get you connected to the person I have in mind. What time suits you best? 10am or midday?"

Never give people more than 2 choices. It confuses people and makes following up difficult. Make it easy for the person you wish to help. If neither of your options work, they will come back to you with options of their own.

"I'm afraid neither of those times will work tomorrow, could you check in with me at 9am or 2?"

Your offer of help or connection will be something of value to them otherwise there would be no need to move anything forward.

Put systems in place that mean you find the time to follow up. It's the easiest step to miss. It's a mistake I have made in the past to my detriment. If the meeting is in the afternoon, set a time in your calendar specifically for following up. If the meeting finishes at 4pm, and you know you can be back in front of your laptop by 6, then put 6–7pm in your calendar and get your follow-ups done.

Give yourself the best opportunity to be a person of integrity in all you do. People who are seen and heard to "do what they say they are going to do" become prized and talked about within the organisation at the levels you want to be talked about.

What systems do you plan to put in place for your networking?

Integrity In Your Network

Choose people of integrity to be your advocates

It's important to make sure that the people in your network have integrity to match yours.

It can be tricky to find ways of measuring integrity when you first meet people. I don't know of anyone who would cast themselves in the role of someone who doesn't have integrity. Humans reveal themselves through their actions rather than words.

I had a friend and work colleague who I considered to be a man of integrity because those around him in my network had assured me, he was. When we first met, I had initial, unconscious misgivings, but I let them go due to the voices from others in my network. For a while this friendship worked out. I did work for his company. For a while, whilst things were going well with his company, he behaved very generously as a person of integrity. When things started to go downhill for him, when the Inland Revenue started investigating his business, he started to reveal himself. To this day, he still owes me money. He always intended to be a man of integrity, but when the chips were down he protected himself and cut people from his network adrift.

There is a reason that contracts are set up to cover the worst of times. Like a first date, people are often on their best behaviour when you first meet, showing the best game face to the world.

Honing a network of people with integrity will take time. There are 4 different types of networker. Here they are:

- Giver
- Taker
- Matcher
- Faker.

We take it as a given that you should be a giver. Surround yourself with fellow givers. Givers are different to Matchers and I shall explain that difference shortly.

Takers are the kind of people you don't want in your network. Takers go networking with a begging hand rather than a giving one. "What can you do for me?" they often ask, taking life to be transactional rather than relational. Takers are more likely to be male than female and more likely to be that direct at the beginnings of a conversation. Of course, you could give a gift of connection to a Taker. My experience of Takers is that they continue to take and nothing is returned. I don't advise that you spend a lot of time with Takers. Be polite but move on as quickly as you can.

Matchers are the trickiest of the types. Matchers mask themselves as Givers. They will offer you something and then wait until you have something for them. If you don't give them something immediately then they are going to let you know about it. I have had Matchers before in my life. Super transactional people.

One Matcher once said to me: "David, I have got a brilliant client for you. I've already sold you. All you have to do is take the money."

How exciting, I thought, thanking this Matcher for their kindness.

I rang this "brilliant client" the next day. She had no idea who I was and no interest in what it was I offered. I was rather befuddled at the end of the call as I had a different expectation of the call.

I went back to my matching friend. "I called that lady you mentioned. She said she never heard of me and didn't want to discuss my services."

"Oh," said my matchmaking friend. "You screwed that up! How did you do that? I had already sold you. Anyway, what have you got for me?"

I've even heard this Matcher speaking to someone else in my network. "I haven't had anything from you in a little while. I mean, you are on the Christmas card list right now. Do you want to be?"

The story I have just told is a pretty extreme kind of Matcher. The principle here is that a gift from a Matcher will not be born of generosity. This is how they reveal themselves. Really they are Takers disguised as Givers. When they are looking at a connection for you, they are really thinking of something for themselves.

When you find yourself in the vicinity of a Matcher in your network give them something in order that they back off from you, and then get them out of your life. They are toxic energy sappers and life is too short to have to deal with that.

The final one is Fakers. Fakers also mask themselves as Givers. A Faker is someone who makes a lot of promises and then nothing ever comes of them. Often a Faker is not as well connected to the people they claim to be as they would like you to think. They big themselves and the perception of their influence up. Often, they give themselves away by offering too many connections all at the same time.

I once had a serious Faker in my network. On paper he looked like an amazing connection if his word was to be believed. Indeed, I did believe him at first. He had a list of 50 people he thought would be the perfect people to introduce me to. He suggested we meet, identify the 10 people I would most like to meet immediately, and then move forward with the introductions.

We arranged to have a one to one. I put 90 minutes aside for this. I was super excited. We had a great session on Skype, sharing screens, working out the best prospects on the list. We ended the meeting after an hour and a half having decided on the 10 best people to introduce me too. I felt that it had been an excellent use of time.

Then, nothing happened. No connections. No follow up emails. Nothing. Days went by. Weeks went by. I rang my contact and got no answer. I rang again and got no answer.

This happened over 3 years ago. He still won't answer when I call.

There is a certain insanity about all of this. To look like he was being generous, this person burned the entirety of our professional relationship because he didn't really have the connections he claimed to. If you are tempted to think I am being a bit judgemental and that there may be other reasons why he did this, then I'd like you to know that a few other people in our mutual network have had the same experience and his reputation in networking circles is toast.

This is why it is important to be of integrity when you operate and surround yourself with people who have integrity too.

The only one of the 4 types of networker who has the integrity to follow through with what they promise is the "Giver". This is why building a long-term relationship is based on the integrity of being someone who offers to help and then does what they say they are going to do.

Be like that and make your core network people like that too.

What Are Your Values?

Live your values through action

How many of us live life though our values? Not many. In my experience it is key to be clear about your values and remind yourself on a daily basis (at least once a day) what they are. Ask yourself honestly whether you fulfilled them in that last engagement of communication you just had.

Many people are cynical about the idea of values. After all, don't all the big corporate organisations hold a set of values that they publish. People are cynical because many of those big corporations don't appear to live up to the values they espouse.

Integrity is a word I have used often, especially in this chapter. "Integrity" is probably the word I have seen most used in a company's set of values. Yet "integrity" is often a word we laugh at because it would appear to the outside world that so few companies who use the word, know what it means.

It is very easy to tell people what your values are. I have sat in boardrooms across Europe where the company has hired an artist to put the "values" in art form on their walls. It is easy to tell people your values. It is a real skill to be able to inhabit them.

Do you remember at the beginning of this book I entreated

you, dear reader, to find out what values people ascribe to you in the job you are in? Have you found them out yet? If not, what have you been doing? Put the book down, go find out what people already value in you, and then come back. Don't forget the bookmark!

Once you know, you can cross these values off your list. People already see them; people already experience them from you.

Now let's look at the values you wish people saw in you but haven't mentioned yet. You want to be in integrity with yourself so choose values that really matter to you. If you run your own business then it can be easier because you just choose. If you are in a role in an organisation, then the values you choose must relate to the values you know the company already espouses.

Take Sir Richard Branson. His top value is "fun". He doesn't do anything unless he is having fun. This value is written into any contract of work he does. It says in the contract: "If Richard is not having any fun, he leaves. No refund will be made available."*

You are likely to have an opinion on this, one way or the other. Good for him, some of you may be saying to yourself. Others might be thinking, "Who the hell does he think he is?"

Regardless of what you think, would you agree that Sir Richard Branson is one of the most influential businesspeople of the last 30 years. He has started well over 25 businesses. Not all of them have been successful. Some of them have been

---

* I put it in quotation marks even though the wording may be slightly different. This is very much the gist of what is written. I know this because 2 of my business mentors paid Sir Richard Branson to come to an event they were putting on for their clients. One of my closest friends went on the trip to the event, which was in Singapore. Sir Richard is one of his heroes, so it was an opportunity he was not about to give up. He told me the day was amazing and that you could see the moment that Sir Richard stopped having fun and tuned out.

super successful (Virgin Records, Virgin Atlantic) and others not so (Virgin Brides anyone?).

Through the process of creating everything he has in life he has stood by the core value of fun. If it wasn't fun, he dropped it. If it was fun, he gave it his all.

He has truly lived his values through action.

If you are working for a company, you may not have the kind of freedom in your values as the CEO of the company. Maybe you can become CEO and change that for yourself.

In the meantime, study the values of the company you work with. Which are the ones they need to see in you? Choose 3 and repeat the exercise in the 2nd chapter of this book when I asked you to think of 3 people who possess these values for you and find out what it is like to inhabit them.

Hold on to those people in your head, and the feeling you had when you inhabited the visualisation of their bodies.

I want you to draw on these visualisation exercises every morning before you go to work.

Getting the best out of your morning is key to how you attack the day.

There is already a perfectly excellent book named *The Miracle Morning* by Hall Ellrod available to get your mornings sorted.

You must make a connection with your values an integral part of your morning routine. If you don't have a morning routine, then it is time you had one. Get out of bed and start the day in the wrong way, or with an unhelpful energy, then that energy affects how you approach everyone. Regardless of how many people and tasks you have around you in the morning you must find time for yourself. I know that women, especially if you are a mum as well, will have a lot of people dependent on them for the morning's access to food and clothing. I totally get that. This may involve getting up a little earlier. Find time for you or nothing will change. You cannot build a sustainable future for yourself unless you are prepared to do something different to the majority.

Thinking about the words in your head is not enough. You must engage the whole body. If ever any of you have seen me live on a stage, you will know that I get my audience engaged fully and physically in taking action. Taking action is the only thing that changes lives.

Write down now all the tasks you perform in the morning before you leave the house or move into a work environment. Be clear and also make sure that every little detail is down.

- Is there anything on that list that could be outsourced?
- Is there anything on that list that you could easily teach someone else in your household to do?
- How much time are you able to create from the above?

If the answer is none, you might want to figure in how much time you need to touch base with your values. Perhaps 15 minutes, perhaps longer. Where can you fit this in?

Make it a routine. By that I mean make sure it happens every day.

The universe is magical. It's a strange thing that the universe rewards us when we take action. The reward we get may not come from the areas we are taking action over, but the reward comes nonetheless. When we take no action, there is no reward.

I was on the phone to a client a couple of days ago who has yet to achieve her promotion. You might expect her to be annoyed with me or upset in some way that the promotion isn't here yet, but nothing could be further from the truth.

The reason she feels "extremely grateful" is the work we have done together has woken her up to her value. She lives it. She inhabits it every day. She thinks of the conversations she speaks up in and the way she stands up for herself against the management who have changed her role in the last 18 months without openly changing it. The woman who first came to me last year to begin work would never have found the courage to step forward and say what she has to say.

She is networking outside of her organisation and has a reputation now, second to none, as the absolute expert on her chosen topic. She is now in a position where she believes that if she is offered a promotion, even with a significant pay increase, then she will think carefully before accepting. She is now on a path to finding freedom and power in everything she does. Her core value is courage and she is living it full time.

Kick-start the best way to live your values, so you live them out in the open, public air and others see them and experience that extra value from you.

Promotion – When You Are Not in the Room

*Do you know what people are saying about
you when you are not in the room?*

Do I have your attention yet? This is the bit where it all comes together.

Promotion. We want you to achieve that promotion. We want you to receive the pay rise that tells you that you are receiving what you are worth.

Remember this mantra – Impact is about what happens when you are in the room. Influence is about what happens when you are not.

For the last 9 chapters we have been focusing on everything you need to be seen, be heard and get paid what you are worth. For some of you it will come reasonably quickly. For others it may take a little longer. It all depends on who you have arguing your corner in the boardroom conversations you are not involved in.

This chapter has been about creating advocacy. Advocacy involves having ambassadors who will articulate your value when you are not there. Those moments when exciting ideas turn up in the boardroom and someone there, without thinking, raises a hand and then says, "Do you know who would be perfect for this?" and then says your name out loud to the big decision makers around company policy, how time is spent, and what you (and everyone else) are paid.

A presentation is often a fast track to getting a promotion. It is a great way to get maximum visibility, especially if you get your presentation video recorded.

The advantage of being a presenter and doing the job well is that you can get an audience of all the best people for you to be in front of, in the one place, at the same time and all focused on you.

Imagine if you could speak to 50 people in one hour instead of having to have 50 one-to-one meetings over a period of 50 hours. That's how to create leverage out of your time.

If it is videoed, then your reach is potentially much further. If people cannot make the presentation you may be able to email them a copy or point to the link on your intranet. Maybe you can arrange a follow up one to one after they have had a chance to view the video.

You can also engage your network, the one you have been spending time developing through this chapter. Perhaps they can forward the video for you. It may be even more powerful if the recommendation comes from another person who believes in you and stands by you.

How else can you use video content to get more visibility and credibility?

There is a super resource called LinkedIn. Do you have a LinkedIn profile yet? If not, get one. Use the principles in this book of how you articulate yourself in your profile.

In corporate circles it is widely believed that if you are on LinkedIn then it means you are in the jobs market and looking for something elsewhere. Your job will be (unless that is true) to counter that by showing your value to your organisation from being on LinkedIn.

Research suggests that it takes 17 different touch points before a customer is willing to talk to a service provider if those touch points happen online.

The same research tells us that watching people on video has a far greater impact on people than looking at photos which has a greater impact than the written word.

The value of connections on LinkedIn are the potential value you can bring into your company. Can you get connected to people who may be big clients or customers? Can you connect to people who may offer value-added services you can give to your own company's clients? Can you find people who would be natural partners for the business you work with?

After all, a core value for any business will be increasing its turnover or upscaling the level of client it works with. Whether you are in sales or not, if you can be seen to be helping that process, over and above the remit of your job, they will have the perception of more value.

Visibility brings promotion. Being seen and heard as a strategic voice brings promotion. You have to stand out from the crowd for people to perceive your value.

Remember the Dunbar number. 160. That is 160–200 (tops) names and faces that the human brain can put together and understand the context of how they know you. Let's assume 160. Be one of the 160. Be seen and be memorable whilst you are being seen. Show them that you are adaptable and someone who has a plan and can formulate a plan. Concentrate on your value. Work on upscaling your value. Get connected to the values of the company that mean something to you. Show those values so the people who pay you can see the alignment.

This is the central idea of this book.

You get paid up to the value that is perceived in you and what you do to solve any company's problem. You want to be paid what you are worth, solve a bigger problem. Solve the problem that is worth the next pay grade.

To be chosen you must be seen and heard.

At the beginning of this book I told you all how one of the biggest banks in the world, when clearing out their house of 1/3 of the staff, fired everyone they felt "had their head down". None of this happens for people because they work harder. It only happens for those who work smarter.

Be one of the smart ones and get yourself the promotion and the money you deserve.

Conclusion

Here we are.

You now have everything you need to be able to change your experience of life and your management's experience of you.

If we were working together then you would have me and the team by your side, to laugh, cry, cajole, celebrate, teach, and coach you to a state of independence. It is one of my greatest satisfactions in life to see a client become the person she wants to be, to know she is rewarded financially to the right level and that she has the respect of her peers and significant influence in the world in which she works.

Of course, we are not working together in a face-to-face way. Yet, I have attempted in this book to imagine that you, dear reader, are someone I am working with closely to get a huge outcome to come home.

I've run through my 3-step system in detail.

Speak – Shine – Make 10 Times the Difference

In 10 chapters we have touched on the detail in this process. Follow the system wherever you come from and whatever industry you work in. Every client has a different story. Every client engagement has, and continues to be, unique. They all have one thing in common. We followed the system together.

First you have to find out how to be present in order to have presence for other people. In finding your presence you find your breath. From there you find your voice and start resonating with the credibility, rapport building and enthusiasm that gets you noticed in a good way.

The next element is the energy you bring to every conversation you have. This is something you can take total charge of. How to do it is in the chapter on energy.

As the Cheshire Cat says in *Alice in Wonderland* "If you don't know where you want to get to, what does it matter which way you go?"

This is why I use the Understand Myself profile to help my clients get a clear idea what it is they would want to be different about them when the process is done.

After you have worked on those elements you are ready to start working on what you articulate and how you articulate it.

The Cat and Dog metaphor is the most fun way of exploring how to build rapport with those you might find it difficult to build rapport with. This is especially useful for building rapport up a management chain.

Have fun playing with the metaphor of Cats and Dogs. Keep it in mind that it is a metaphor. Don't take it too seriously. Develop your powerful Cat. Develop your rapport building to a higher level with more judicious use of the Dog.

Impact is about what happens when you are in the room. Influence is about what happens when you are not. (Not again, I hear you cry! Yes, again!) What influence you have is dependent on what impact you have.

Knowledge is never enough. You have to be motivated to take action. Motivation doesn't last, which is why we recommend you have some daily. Working on your mindset will change that. That is why I have devoted so many pages here to helping you to transform how you approach every day of your life. Time is the real commodity here, not money.

The truth about money is not widely known. We all carry a number of stories in our heads around money and what it means to have money. If the full amount of money in the world was equally distributed around every individual in the world, it would be back in the pockets of the same people who have it now within a month. The reason is the stories that most people hold in their minds around money. Most people's stories will tell them to get rid of that money as quickly as possible. Perhaps this is a new idea, perhaps it is not. If it is new to you then I am thankful I was the person who can help you change this. If you have read or heard from some of the amazing mentors I have consulted over the years in my own life, like Robert Kiyosaki and his brilliant *Rich Dad, Poor Dad* book, then I still advise you to look to the exercises I have revealed in the money chapter here. So many lives have dramatically changed because of the 3 Chair exercise. Make yours the next one to change.

No human being is an island. The self-made millionaire is an apocryphal tale that is plainly not true. Every success story has a network of advocates who recognise their potential value as well as their value and helped manoeuvre them into position. Everyone needs mentors. It is my most sincere hope that this book has been a form of mentorship, limited I know in comparison to a real human engagement, that makes a difference to you.

I've not mentioned my own core values in the writing of this book. I'd like to finish by talking about one of them.

One of my core values is to leave people in a better place than I found them. Whatever state people arrive at my door (or virtual door as has mainly been the case for the last 18 months), my intention is always to leave them better when they go. That intention has been at the forefront of my mind when deciding to write this book and in deciding what goes in. I hope that you find my intention has been fulfilled.

If this book makes you feel in some way curious to find out more then perhaps you might like to have a conversation. The team and I are super engaged with our clients. However, we would like to find time for everyone who needs us. That is why I am happy to offer a 45-minute complimentary strategic coaching call to anyone who makes contact via email saying they read this book. So you have some context here, I charge my private clients £750 for a 45-minute coaching call. It will be with a member of the Speak to Shine team. Our promise is that we will not use that time to sell to you. Our promise is that we will use that time to make sure you leave us in a better space than you arrive. If we think, after that call, we might be a good fit to help you achieve a specific outcome, we can discuss that then.

If you think that might be a valuable use of time for you then email me here – david@davidroylance.com – and we will respond.

Serving you as I write this book has been a pleasure. I wish you the most amazing success with what you find within it.

Yours

David A Roylance

Bonus Chapter:
Your Relationship With Yourself

The Long Dark Night of the Soul

Are you prepared to look in the mirror?

If you have picked up this book because you want to change the circumstances of your life then it is likely that your relationship with yourself is not the best it could be.

In order to grow our income or our assets we need to start with ourselves. We need to know where, what and who we are; otherwise, how will we know who we need to become to get the things we want in life?

In this book I will be concentrating more on telling my own story of development rather than the stories of clients I shared in my last book. Several times in my life I have found myself taking the trip down into the long dark night of the soul, staring down the mirror and facing every aspect of who I was then and what needed to change. It is part of the human condition to want to achieve and create more with the short time we have here. I wish I had known that much earlier than I did in life.

If you were not already aware, I was a drama student in the early 1990s at the Guildhall School of Music and Drama. The school is based in the Barbican Centre and was a real hotbed of creating, competitive and with sexual energy. It's a simple truth that when you put 26 creatively minded people in an enclosed space that there will be a lot of emotional and physical desire and energy shared between said people.

I was in my late 20s when I went there. I moved down to London from Scotland in 1990. Although I had lived away from my parents for 9 years in Edinburgh and been involved in the theatre scene for all of that time, this is the first time I had lived outside of Scotland.

I had the most amazing training at the Guildhall. Our building was right next to the Barbican Centre itself. We were 2 minutes walk from an auditorium where we could see the finest actors of our generation being directed by some of the finest directors. The Barbican also was a centre of excellence for theatre from across the globe. It was at the Edinburgh Festival that I discovered my love of theatre from across the globe. With the Barbican being moments away from my daily life, I got access to the finest international theatre, on a monthly basis at least.

I don't think back a great deal to this time. Thinking about it now, there is a thrill in my blood that reminds me of the heightened emotional state I was in for the majority of the 3 years.

It was in my second year that the pressure being applied truly began to hit home. I found a level of exhaustion that I have never experienced before. I also found an extraordinarily passionate love with someone I absolutely should not have. She was from the other side of the world, and she already had a partner. My desire got the better of my common sense and after inviting her for a Sunday afternoon lunch and wander around Hampstead Heath, we found ourselves in a relationship.

To quote another much greater writer than I, "It was the best of times, it was the worst of times." (*A Tale of Two Cities*, by Charles Dickens.)

Because of the complicated nature of this relationship, we would break up and get back together on a weekly basis. I kid you not. We would often have the most wonderful weekends together, then break up on Sunday night only to be back together, tentatively, on Tuesday. We would see each other hourly in the drama corridor. To add to the pressure, we were also attempting (rather poorly – and rather over dramatically) to keep this relationship a secret from everyone else in our years.

I'm sure you can imagine the emotional pressure going on. Boom and bust, emotionally speaking. I was super competitive. I was because I was determined to win her. I gave this relationship my all.

The strain of being in and out of a relationship every week began to show and my work as a developing actor suffered. My sleep cycle was a mess, and I was finding it difficult to concentrate. There was also a good deal of guilt that I was in a relationship that had to be kept a secret because, essentially, we were cheating a man on the other side of the world who had no idea I existed.

It culminated one morning (a Monday I think it was) as I was coming out of the Barbican tube and was stopped by a particularly officious ticket inspector. I lost control of myself. I blew a fuse very publicly during rush-hour in front of hundreds of people, left the station, rammed my foot into the wall of a neighbouring bank and screamed. Luckily, I had one of my housemates with me who calmed me down and took me into college.

I turned to my first mentor, Patsy Rodenburg. I remember having a conversation with her outside of the Barbican entrance during a sunny Spring day.

If you have read "Be Seen, Be Heard, Get Paid What You Are Worth" you will know that Patsy was the first mentor I had in life.

If you haven't then let me tell you that Patsy Rodenburg is the world's number one voice coach. She is also the world's number one expert on William Shakespeare. What she does not know about Shakespeare is not worth knowing.

I mention this because the works of William Shakespeare are unique. All life is represented in his plays and his sonnets. Any experience you name can be found in Shakespeare.

Patsy went above and beyond with me when I was at my most vulnerable. I wept freely when I was telling her of my experience.

She referenced the poem "Long Dark Night of the Soul" by St John of the Cross. This idea of facing yourself in a spiritual crisis is often referred to as the Long Dark Night of the Soul. It intimates that the crisis is temporary. It may last a long time, or not.

I needed to take a good long look at myself in a mirror. I mean metaphorically rather than physically. I needed to find out whether I liked myself or not. If I didn't, then how do I change that? If I cannot like myself then how do I end the suffering I was visiting on myself?

It was the first time I was aware of the idea that I, myself, and myself only, was responsible for all the pain I was putting into my life. Up to that point I was happy to point the finger of blame at the woman who was constantly breaking and mending my heart. No, I was totally responsible for my own mess.

I remember one afternoon being in the café area within Guildhall talking to my friends, in a state of exhaustion, and being aware – almost like a hallucinatory experience – of a mirror (that was entirely in my own mind) and seeing myself in that mirror. The rest of the world around me went into a soft focus. I stopped listening to whatever was being said and expressed all the pain, anger and anguish that I needed to express.

Moments later it was done and I felt an enormous weight lift from me.

That weekend my girlfriend broke up with me on a Sunday night over the phone. She called me back on Monday to restart the relationship. I took responsibility and said "No". It was painful, and it remained painful for months. We never got back together again. What I had discovered was that I liked myself and I was worth better than the way I was allowing myself to be treated.

Carl Jung's *The Shadow*

The Enemy Within

Most of us are held back by our fears that come to us disguised as thoughts suggesting we are being good.

Every story has a hero and a villain. In your story you are both.

If you say that you will never, under any circumstance, be an aggressive person then you are being a coward.

Sounds pretty harsh, right? I'm imaging that statement might be an emotional trigger for many reading it. Stay with those emotions for a moment. What are they? Recognise them. Stay with them. Be honest about what they are. Is there a desire for aggression within that?

I'm going to come back to that later.

The Gothic writers of the 19th Century had real insight into the psychology of the human spirit. The story of Deacon Brodie, in Edinburgh, was a major influence on Robert Louis Stevenson when he wrote *Dr Jekyll and Mr Hyde*. The mythic quality of this story is recognisable to everybody who experiences life. How do we strive to be good? What do I do about those thoughts and feelings you (and I) find ourselves experiencing in life, and would rather we didn't?

William Brodie was one of the most well-respected members of Edinburgh society during the 18th Century. He was a gifted cabinet maker, locksmith, and Head of (Deacon of) the Incorporation of Wrights and Masons. Unbeknownst to anyone in the Incorporation he also had a night-time occupation as the head of a ring of very successful burglars. He genuinely had a double life. The hauls he made with his successful burglaries allowed him to have an extravagant night-time lifestyle. He had at least 2 mistresses. He had fathered numerous children. He had a very expensive gambling habit.

It was the gambling habit that really undid him. He got cocky, copied the locks of his customers and then robbed them in the night. Things went spectacularly wrong when he planned a raid on His Majesty's Excise office in central Edinburgh. Although Brodie escaped to Holland, many of his men were captured and turned on Brodie, giving evidence against him. Brodie was arrested in Amsterdam and returned to Edinburgh where he was tried and found guilty. He was sentenced to death by hanging. He was hanged on a gibbet he had designed himself. That irony would be one worthy of a blockbuster Hollywood movie.

It is a great story and an inspiration for Jekyll and Hyde. The Gothic writers in the 19th Century, working alongside the birth of psychoanalysis, were focused on the duality of humanity. The fact that there are opposing psychological forces working inside each one of us. In Jekyll and Hyde's case the separation of these 2 forces became the undoing of the man.

Carl Jung is one of the most important names of the early 20th Century. His contribution to the world resulted in people being able to analyse their lives significantly more deeply than they had ever done before. Without him there may never have been a personal development movement.

Originally, he worked under Sigmund Freud. However, their ideas diverged when Jung began to feel that Freud's ideas were far too simple.

Jung identified that there are a series of universal patterns in the unconscious mind. He identified 12 in total. He called these patterns "archetypes". An archetype is a series of repeated patterns of behaviour.

The archetype we have the most interest in here is "The Shadow". The Shadow is the archetype that deals with desire, sex and life choices. The Shadow is the representation of everything you know exists within you, yet you are afraid to see or recognise it. The Shadow is the opposite of the "Persona". The Persona is the image of us we present to the world. The Persona is the version of us we would like others to see.

I love the idea of The Shadow as a name for these behaviours. The Shadow cannot exist if there is no light. How much light there is defines the Shadow for you. Where light shines from defines the size of the Shadow. The Shadow looms over us all, becoming greater for those of us who refuse to see that it is there. The Shadow is every thought and desire that any of us have had that we regret and wish we had not thought or felt. Any desire to do violence or wish for something that so-called moral society would not approve of.

Think of the Persona as our desire to be seen as harmless. Think of the Shadow as our potential to be dangerous.

Which brings me back to that original sentence at the top of this section.

If you say that you will never, under any circumstance, be an aggressive person then you are being a coward.

If there is nothing in this world you care about enough to be aggressive in their defence, then what use are you to anyone you claim to love and care for?

Harmless is the worst thing a human being can be, if they want to make the world, or even just their own world, a better place. To be dangerous is to be capable of making your mark in this world. To be harmless is to be invisible.

The world is littered with sad stories of the people who were unable to reconcile their Shadow. Often with men in their 40s it is referred to as "the mid-life crisis". In this case, men attempt to hold in the feelings and desires they are fearful of others knowing until the pressure cooker explodes and they destroy the life they have carefully cultivated until this point. Rather than look in, face their demons and incorporate their Shadow into their life, they absolve their demons to the care of alcohol, drugs and all manner of so-called addictions.

Every single one of us on this planet has a Shadow. If we fail to recognise and reconcile ourselves to the Shadow, then we run the risk of never being useful – at least to the degree that we wish we were in this world.

The work of incorporating the Shadow is often difficult work. It is extremely rewarding. What that work looks like is up to you. It is your Shadow, after all.

Agreeableness is the personality aspect that most sinks the prospects of those who come to work with me. Be too agreeable, you will be walked upon by those who aren't.

Assimilate your Shadow.

Who Depends on You?

Your influence may be bigger than you think

Let's face it, you are not going to be "feeling it" every day. There are going to be some mornings when you won't feel up to doing the work that needs to be done to ensure you have a different experience of life to the majority.

The work I describe in the section above around finding your Shadow and incorporating it into who you are is going to be gnarly work. It is going to be an uncomfortable and sometimes exhausting period of growth. There are going to be mornings when you wake up and won't feel like doing the work. There will be days when you don't feel like going the extra mile. You will look at others who don't share your desires to go the extra mile and wonder "why should I" today.

It happens to us all, despite the passion with which we declare we won't.

How do we deal with this when it happens for us?

This is the reason a person should incorporate their shadow into their life. With your Shadow by your side, properly controlled and channelled, what is possible for you increases tenfold. The Shadow side of you will show up when you are tired, when things go wrong and when you feel overwhelmed.

It will attach itself to your fears if you haven't welcomed your Shadow into you.

We must have something bigger than us that sustains us during those moments.

No one is an island. Life is defined by our interconnection with others.

Love is always the answer. Who do you love? Who do you love who depends on you?

This is often an easy answer for those of us who have children. For those who don't then, scan further afield to find the people in your life who benefit from your existence and presence and who would miss you if you were not there. Who would benefit in your life if you sustained your energy and went that extra mile on those days you don't feel like it, or are tempted to surrender to fear?

Write a list now. Who depends on you? Who do you love?

Find photographs of the people on your list. Place those pictures on the desk at which you work, or on the wall (like a vision board). Make sure these photographs are in your eyeline as you work.

The next time you wake up not in the mood, or feeling ill, or in fear of taking action, take some time to look at the pictures of those you love and ask yourself this question:

"Are you prepared to tell these people you do not love them enough to go the extra mile?" Imagine how it would feel to tell them this. How are they likely to react? What emotions flood through your body when you imagine that scenario?

Use the feeling this creates in your body to step over whatever makes you feel like not making the effort. Get used to using this visualisation in your arsenal.

I'd like to link the ethos of connecting to those you love

and your connections with the rest of the world. Therefore, when I was talking about the Shadow, I talk about people being cowardly if they refuse to onboard the aspects of their personality they do not like.

It is imperative that you do this work on yourself, and honestly too, because you are not an island. You do not exist in isolation. All human beings are interconnected. For some of us there are animals too!

Love Yourself to Love Others

Love Your Neighbour as You
Would Love Yourself

The Bible entreats us to love our neighbour as we would love ourselves. This implicitly suggests that it is best to love oneself because it makes it possible to love your neighbour.

As a culture we shy away from the idea of self-love. Too "woo-woo" for many of us. It is also a fear that people have that if we love ourselves, it might turn us into narcissists.

Let's clear this up once and for all. Loving yourself and narcissism are completely different experiences of life. The narcissist may appear on the surface to love themselves. Nothing could be further from the truth. The narcissist moves life and the people in their lives around the chess board of life like pawns who exist only for the purpose of their own self-interest. The narcissist is driven by a lack of regard for others. Those who focus on loving themselves do so with the express purpose of giving more to others and benefitting those around them.

Maslow suggests that love is impossible without self love. If you cannot love yourself, whatever you claim to be love for others cannot be such a thing. In his hierarchy of needs he places self-actualisations as the highest of all needs, the need to actualise in the world all that you can possibly be. This actualisation is impossible without self-love.

The 5 elements of self love (known as The Constructs of Self Love) are:

- Self Knowledge
- Self Acceptance
- Self Being
- Self Transcendence
- Self Renewal.

Self Knowledge

Let's begin with Self Knowledge.

The idea that one should "know oneself" is an idea as old as the Greek philosophers and equally in the eastern philosophies.

The mistake that many of us make is thinking that knowing oneself is simply understanding one's personality. If that were the case, then the personality assessment I use with my private clients would be enough to solve all problems.

We must dig deeper and understand our "spirit" or what the ancient Greeks called the "daimon". Knowing yourself from within inspires self-love. Attempting to find the answer from outside yourself will inspire narcissism.

Self Acceptance

To accept yourself, healthily, is a must in the journey to actualising self-love in the world. To be in a state of self acceptance is to be less afraid of the world, less afraid of judgement and not, in any way, afraid of what other people may say or think about you. Self acceptance also dispels the need for "perfection" in any aspect of your life. Any criticism or feedback you receive will be assimilated without indulgence.

Self Being

Often in life we are drawn like a moth to a flame by the idea of security and safety being offered by the herd and complying with the demands of the herd. In those conditions you cannot get yourself to a position of self love because you care about the herd and its approval. You are also afraid of the separateness that being openly yourself in the world would cause. Historically, the herd have never appreciated originality and newness, so there will certainly be some form of rejection from the herd as self-actualisation. Self-actualisation was defined by Maslow as "the individual becoming everything they are capable of becoming". This would mean, according to the individual, articulating all of your talents to the world. Self-actualisation is the highest of Maslow's hierarchy of needs. Think of people who have "their own style" as they appear in the world. These people have reached the stage of self being.

Self Transcendence

Self-Transcendence is described as the ability to move being the consciousness of self-centredness. This is not the idea of "giving up of the self". On the contrary this is the idea of transcending the ego of self and understanding our connectedness in the world. "Love oneself in the context of the greater world". In many ways it is a call for an individual to actualise their leadership potential to the world. In Africa there is a concept called Ubuntu – the idea that "I am because you are". This is the point that self-love explores the idea of loving your neighbour. As Jesus entreats, "Love Yourself As

You Love Your Neighbour" meaning to think of yourself as someone worthwhile as you would your neighbour.

Self Renewal

Self renewal is about your ability to nourish yourself physically, mentally, spiritually, and emotionally. "You cannot pour from an empty cup" or the other expression "You can't jump start another car if your own battery is empty" are metaphors for this idea which is continuous professional and personal development in your life. Can you care about yourself enough to recognise when you need nourishment in any of those areas and have the discipline to make sure you get that nourishment?

The reason there is so little self love at the top tables of many organisations is that the idea is misunderstood. Because many people think that narcissism and self-love are the same thing, they avoid delving into the powerful possibilities inherent in the idea.

Where there is narcissism there is NO love. Be clear about this for yourself so you can be clear when you encounter it. Self-love is the only weapon to counter it and stop a narcissist impacting on your life, professionally or personally.

The Voices

Which voices? Yes, those ones

Society tends to demonise the idea of hearing voices in our head, and if you are hearing voices other than your own attempting to give you instruction or criticism then I suggest contacting the charitable organisation I supported for many years, MIND.

Every one of us has voices in our own head. They are all our own voices. They are all different areas of us. We need these voices to make sense of the world. We need these voices to rationalise the information that comes to us from the rest of the world. Is what I am listening to true? Is this the only interpretation of what I am seeing unfolding? What is this feeling?

These voices can also be a defence mechanism that self sabotages our opportunities to head out of our comfort zone. Who reading this can resonate with the idea of a voice in our own head telling us "I am not good enough!" "You will never do this?" "Who do you think you are?" I think most reading this will have experienced this in a lifetime. It is part of the process of being human.

As I explored in the previous section, the desire for security and safety within the herd is strong.

If you like, the voices in your head are your 3rd Eye. I have heard it called less complimentary words ("little fxxxer" as an old friend of mine from the world of the theatre used to call it) for instance. I think to denigrate the voice is to misunderstand its purpose and value. For we all have within us the capacity to train this voice to work for us and our greater good, rather than against us.

I would love all of you reading this to have your strategies for taming the voice and turning the voices into an asset for you.

Our physical experience defines our mental and emotional experience. The heart rate defines how much oxygen sits in the frontal lobe of the brain. The oxygen in the frontal lobe defines whether a human being is in fight or flight mode or not.

The oxygen in our frontal lobe defines also whether the voices work for us or against us.

Here are some methods for keeping ourselves out of "fight or flight" so we can have the best use of the voices in our head.

1. Breathing – You have to be breathing in the stomach to have a fully oxygenated brain. If you are breathing

in the chest, slow your breath down and release into the stomach.

2. Energy – when we are in a fight or flight scenario the blood retreats in the system to protect the vital organs. We feel colder as a result and the energy we face the world with changes. When we are nervous, our energy is low. When we are comfortable it is high. Changing your energy will shift the voice that is in charge.

3. Exercise – shift your physical energy, change your mental and emotional energy, change the voices. Start your day with 30 minutes of physical exercise to nourish your body, and you'll nourish the rest of your day.

4. Music – What are your favourite pieces of music that make you feel great? Compile a list on whatever device you use and have them to hand for whenever you need them to shift energies.

5. Smells – Let's not forget that as sensual creatures all the senses come into play to affect our mood. During the lockdown I shared my office with my wife for the fitness classes she delivered to her own audience. She delivered high energy cardio workouts and dance classes to her audience regularly. She also, thoughtfully, had a series of candles to hand for the immediate hour after her session so I could still work with passion and clarity with my own clients.

6. Stop watching television – especially the news. I know many of my clients feel they need to stay plugged into the news and watch last thing at night before heading to bed. Not surprisingly they have a poor night's sleep and low energy the next day. Most of our modern problems come from a state of abundance rather than scarcity. Children attached to a device all day become obese and unable to form relationships in adulthood. The fact that we can watch television or play games online 24/7 is an abundance that is as detrimental to the human experience as is a diet of pure sugar.

7. Get 8 hours sleep! Simple instruction. I don't think it needs an explanation.
8. Practice daily the idea of gratitude. What are you grateful for in your life? Focus on what you do have and value rather than that which you do not.
9. Dance! Perhaps this should go directly after Music in the list. Dance your energy into the world. Choose your favourite pieces of music and dance like no one is watching (because they are not). Dance like no one is watching anyway, even if they are. Forget what others may think.
10. Connect to another human being who will raise us up. Too often we become limited in our thinking and experience in life because of our community. Find a community that will raise you up by offering a higher level of energy.
11. Offer to help someone. Lend a hand to a neighbour.

I hope you find this list useful. Choose you favourites and make sure you use them as a system. If you are going to do 30 minutes of exercise to kick off your day then make sure it is a "must" in your life.

Any of the above will transform the quality of voice in your head, opening up possibilities rather than closing down options.

Outer and Inner Confidence

Where would you like to begin?

There are 2 different types of confidence. Outer confidence, which is what you show the outside world, and inner confidence, where you feel confident on the inside and your internal conversation (yes, those voices again) reflect your confidence.

Outer Confidence is the easiest of the 2 to achieve. You model the behaviours of confidence using your body. Amy Cuddy has her superb video on adopting power poses. In a sustained power pose, imagine yourself as Wonder Woman or Superman.

Inner Confidence is the trickier to achieve because it is for your own benefit and no other. Who are you when you are on your own? Are you the same confident power posing super-star that you are in front of others?

This is a key indication of how genuine your confidence is. Do you have to put on an act when others are with you or are you the same person when alone as you are in company?

Rather than publish a list of how to make this happen for you, I suggest you go back over the previous sections in this chapter. That is if you still think it a mystery how to find your inner confidence. Everything given in this chapter will help you find it.

Instead, I want to tell you how this has been my journey. It has been the journey I have been on through childhood and my early life as an adult. It is a story through the years that I desperately sought to be accepted by communities and worked to be recognised as worthwhile.

As I look back it seems crazy that I found it so difficult to do that. The risks of being "uncool" or making a mistake felt so great. When I did make mistakes (and I made many) I would internally flagellate myself with those voices.

As a young actor I fought against the belief system that I wasn't good enough. Of course, on a conscious level I didn't believe it. The unconscious mind left me sabotaging oppor-tunity after opportunity in my theatrical life.

I kept switching what I wanted to do with life every 4 or 5 years. After spending 3 years of my life training at one of the top 3 (recognised globally) professional acting schools and working with some of the finest teachers in the world, alongside 4 of the most recognised successful actors working today, I chose to direct and so abandoned my acting career before giving it a chance.

I worked hard as a director without understanding the stories I was telling myself about money and about deserving money. I had no idea that money was a benevolent influence. My feelings of malevolence kept money away from me.

I became a coach without knowing anything about running a business. I pretended I was running a business when in fact I was an associate of 2 companies meaning I had none of the protections that employment would have given me and all of the downsides. I worked 5, sometimes 6, days a week travelling across the country, and occasionally abroad, at the client's behest, believing that this was me running my business.

By then I had achieved outer confidence. I could fake confidence at any stage. I could actively be confident in delivering my work. I took genuine pleasure in serving clients. I could fly and shine when I was on that "stage".

When I came home after being onstage, I disappeared into my shell and hid. When I was alone, I was another person. The voices in my head grew strong, especially at 3.58 in the morning when I would wake in a cold sweat with worry about the future.

Having children gave me strength. I moved out of London and into a large townhouse on the day my son was born. Initially I found confidence. That confidence was shattered when the second dip of the recession hit in 2011. I collapsed under the weight of responsibility at that time. The voice in my head drove me to believe I was worth more to my family dead than alive. For a while, I considered this as a real choice.

I've spoken before about the long dark night of the soul. Here it was again. I was facing the idea that this day, the day I got out of bed that morning, would be the last day on Earth for me.

On that day I found inner confidence in what I thought, at the time, was cowardice. I found the confidence to carry on.

There was no magic realisation of something I had missed. There was no solution discovered as if in a Hollywood film. When I walked back to my car to carry on living and take responsibility for my life, I was in exactly the same state as when I walked away from my car into the woods with 2 packets of paracetamol.

I beg of you to believe in yourself. I beg you to have inner confidence. I beg you to master that voice and train it to be a genuine, not an unremitting critic. The value you bring to the world is immense if you let yourself bring it. You can only do that if you resonate in the world. You can only do that if you connect with people. You can only do that if you offer something that others value. Which is something you do. You may not know what it is you offer, yet. You may not yet know the right people to offer it to. None of that matters. If you haven't found it, keep looking.

Resources the Author Recommends

Thomas Mansfield LLP

With vast experience in dealing with directors, partners, NEDs, finance, legal and HR personnel across a wide range of industries, when it comes to protecting your position within an organisation and maximising your earning potential you can rely on our employment solicitors to provide practical solutions.

Thomas Mansfield Employment Law Solicitors
www.thomasmansfield.com
+44 (0)20 7377 2829
info@thomasmansfield.com

Lucy Long

Many of my clients share their concerns about what happens to them and their families if they find themselves ill or injured. If you recognise that thought, then I would advise you to speak to someone who has helped me know that I and my family are completely secure and able to get immediate attention whatever should happen.

Please meet Lucy Long.

Lucy has her own business, but works with the Western Provident Association (WPA) and has looked after my family beautifully over the last 6 years. I have recommended her to many of my clients and wholeheartedly do so here too. Surprisingly, I don't pay for her services or pay more with WPA for having her.

Feel free to contact Lucy at lucy.long@hcp-plc.org.uk

or +44 (0)7990 600789

if you want to discuss insurance for you or your company health insurer cover – I am 100% sure you will be thanking me for the introduction if you decide to do so.

The Innovation Partnership

Many of my clients have found that upscaling their networking by being in a room with like-minded people makes a huge difference to their prospects. If you are dedicated to innovating within your career and also your impact to the world then I recommend The Innovation Partnership to you. If this sounds attractive to you, please contact Corina Balaneanu at:

corina@innovationpartnership.co.uk

Take One TV

Getting more visibility in the world is key to providing more value. One of the ways my clients create visible leverage to the world and upscale their credibility is through the use of professional video content.

I recommend Take One TV as the go to place if you want great videos.

Email Karen Pawlowska at:

karen@takeonetv.com

Joanna Polak-Goodman – Image Talks

In this book we talk about refining your skills so that you are seen and heard. The next natural step in this process in ensuring that the visual messages that you send are in alignment with your skills and abilities. Wearing the right colours, glasses and wearing clothing and accessories to flatter your proportions and reflect both your personality and your expertise, can help you convey your personal message, but if you get it wrong this can distract and destroy your personal impact! I know how important this is from personal experience.

Joanna Polak-Goodman from

www.imagetalks.eu

is a leading International Corporate Image Consultant and Personal Brand Coach. She is a true talent in this field, as well as being really personable and fun. She fuses her many years of Directorship-level roles running large client-facing teams in the financial sector together with her Image Consultancy Expertise to ensure that her clients achieve congruence between how they look and their personal attributes.

Contact her via Linkedin: https://www.linkedin.com/in/joannapolakgoodman/

or her website

www.imagetalks.eu

for a confidential 20-minute chat to learn how to transform your image to reflect your expertise.

Busy Life PA

A lot of my clients have PAs who are massively overworked and struggling to do everything. For those clients I recommend Stephanie Marco of Busy Life PA, the PA to PAs. Stephanie and her team will offload your PA of all the tasks around taking care of your personal life giving you back hours of time.

Please contact Stephanie

on +44 (0)7956 284788

or Stephanie@busylifepa.co.uk.

Simon Rogers – The Mind/Body Coach

During the 6-month process that my clients experience, it is often the case that those clients need to recognise, understand and assimilate their feelings in order to change the results they are getting in life, and to be happier in being themselves.

When that is the case, I often get them working with my colleague Simon Rogers, the Mind/Body Coach.

I recommend Simon to anyone reading this book who might be asking questions about their emotions or why they are thinking in an unhelpful way.

Simon can be contacted here

at +44 (0)7858244410

or by email at: simon@restoreyourbodynow.co.uk.

Printed in Great Britain
by Amazon

21590722R00130